A Walk through the BIBLE *in* MODERN PARABLES

To Joey and Silena,

May your walk through life be abundantly blessed!

Sincerely,
Clyde Wilkins-Carter Sr.

Also by Clyde Willis Cutrer Sr.

SON OF FROG POND
Tales of the Not-So-Hot Preacher from the Swamp

FROG POND
Millennial Tales and More

A Walk through the BIBLE in MODERN PARABLES

Clyde Willis Cutrer Sr.

Providence House Publishers
Franklin, Tennessee

Copyright 2001 by Clyde Willis Cutrer Sr.

All rights reserved. Written permission must be secured from the publisher to use or reproduce any part of this book, except for brief quotations in critical reviews or articles.

Printed in the United States of America

05   04   03   02   01   1   2   3   4   5

Library of Congress Catalog Card Number: 00-110729

ISBN: 1-57736-215-2

Cover design by Gary Bozeman

All Scripture quotations, unless otherwise indicated, are taken from the Revised Standard Version of the Bible, copyright 1952 [2nd edition, 1971] by the Division of Christian Education of the National Council of the Churches of Christ in the United States of America. Used by permission. All rights reserved.

Scripture quotations marked (NRSV) are taken from the New Revised Standard Version Bible, copyright 1989, Division of Christian Education of the National Council of the Churches of Christ in the United States of America. Used by permission. All rights reserved.

PROVIDENCE HOUSE PUBLISHERS
238 Seaboard Lane • Franklin, Tennessee 37067
800-321-5692
www.providencehouse.com

A class in *Introduction to the Bible* was included in the course load I taught for several years at Belmont University in Nashville. There it was my good fortune to share the thoughts of many inquisitive and bright students. One particular semester, several nursing students called to my attention the beginning signs of a heart attack I wasn't even aware I was having. To those students, and to their many classmates through the years, I thankfully dedicate this little layman's sketch of the Bible.

Contents

PREFACE AND ACKNOWLEDGMENTS   xi

PART 1   THE OLD TESTAMENT

1.	Beginnings	Genesis	3
2.	Departures and Delays	Exodus	6
3.	To Worship	Leviticus	9
4.	Is that a Donkey Lying in Your Path?	Numbers	11
5.	Is God Out to Get You?	Deuteronomy	14
6.	Aiming High	Joshua	17
7.	Avoiding Dark Ages	Judges	19
8.	The Ark and Four-Leaf Clovers	1 & 2 Samuel	22
9.	Worship in a Giant Insect-Exploding World	1 & 2 Kings	24
10.	A 3x5 Glossy with No Flaws, Please	1 & 2 Chronicles	26
11.	If It Had Been a Snake	Amos	28
12.	Unexpected Developments	Hosea	31
13.	In Quietness and Confidence	Isaiah	33

14.	The Importance of Verbs	Micah	35
15.	Over Marriage's Thresholds	Zephaniah	37
16.	Straightening Leaning Towers	Nahum	39
17.	Why Did You Do That, God?	Habakkuk	41
18.	In the Palm of His Hand	Jeremiah	43
19.	Moving On	Lamentations	45
20.	Spitting Out Sour Grapes	Ezekiel	47
21.	A Reassuring Presence	2 Isaiah	49
22.	When Two and Two Do Not Make Four	Haggai	52
23.	A Snapshot of a Golden Age	Zechariah	55
24.	Commerce and Caring	Ezra	57
25.	Jump-Starting Life	Nehemiah	59
26.	A Gratitude Party	Malachi	61
27.	The Opportunity of a Dilemma	Proverbs	63
28.	Suffering's Extended Shelf Life	Job	65
29.	A Meaningful Life	Ecclesiastes	67
30.	Love Songs	Song of Songs	69
31.	Exercises in Remembering	Psalms	71
32.	Toward Healing	Obadiah	73
33.	Building Resolve	Joel	75
34.	Hopelessness Dispelled	Daniel	77
35.	Including Outsiders	Esther	79
36.	Nitty-Gritty Love	Ruth	81
37.	Not a Vanity Plate	Jonah	83

PART 2 THE NEW TESTAMENT

38.	Emerging from the Shadows	Mark	87
39.	So Many Choices	Matthew	90
40.	A Hymn-Singing Church	Luke	93
41.	Present Blessings	John	96
42.	The Miracle of Hope	Acts	98
43.	A Determined Decision	Romans	100

44.	Troubles Abound	1 Corinthians	102
45.	Sufficient Grace	2 Corinthians	104
46.	Appreciating Guides	Galatians	107
47.	Responsible Relationships	Ephesians	109
48.	Looking Up	Philippians	112
49.	Cosmic Glue	Colossians	114
50.	Resilience in Faith	1 Thessalonians	116
51.	No Freeloaders	2 Thessalonians	118
52.	Offense for Life's Blows	1 Timothy	120
53.	Disabled and Enabled	2 Timothy	122
54.	The Spirit and the Letter	Titus	124
55.	To Be Useful	Philemon	126
56.	Running on Empty	Hebrews	128
57.	Rags, Riches, and Religion	James	131
58.	Grace and Blame	1 Peter	134
59.	The Effort to Live	2 Peter	136
60.	Facing the Storm	1 John	138
61.	A Neighborly Billboard	2 John	140
62.	Doing Good	3 John	141
63.	The Keeper	Jude	143
64.	The Victory	Revelation	145

About the Author   148

Preface & Acknowledgments

Parables or stories are often included in books and lectures. Speakers sometimes make their most memorable remarks through anecdotes or stories. This does not defeat their purpose, of course. Just the opposite is true. Stories are the windows that throw light upon the subject. To remember the story is to remember the subject.

A walk through the Bible can be challenging for the lay reader. But if telling modern parables raises the windows from Genesis to Revelation, the walk may be more easily remembered.

Moreover, if the stories tie the parts of the Bible together, the walk can be even more significant. Instead of viewing books as bits and pieces of the Bible, hopefully the completed picture can be seen.

The material in this volume is arranged in brief chapters, allowing the reader to become familiar with a single part of the Bible at a time. Old Testament books are arranged in a nontraditional, more chronological order. These short chapters enable the reader to reflect upon the meaning of the part as it engages the reader's life. The purpose is to objectively and briefly sketch the books of the Bible, including their relationship to the whole, to undergird the reader's devotional reflections. Reading a chapter a day, the book may be used as a tool for daily devotions.

This book seeks to objectively clarify the material upon which one's particular religious position may rest. My comments as the writer are meant to provide universal spiritual nourishment.

Part 1

THE OLD TESTAMENT

> "Create in me a clean heart, O God, and put a new and right spirit within me. Restore to me the joy of thy salvation and uphold me with a willing spirit."
> Psalm 51:10, 12

Chapter One
BEGINNINGS

A major theme of Genesis is beginnings. The beauty of beginnings is that they can be repeated. And they can be repeated after failure. A case in point can be seen in the experience of an admired friend. Floyd Dean Sr. was a good man, a kind and gracious deacon in his church in Kentwood, Louisiana. In his later years, the beloved Floyd was referred to as Pa by his family, and the lovely Mrs. Dean was called Nanny. When they traveled with their good friends Berlin and Pauline Bryant, Berlin would sit in the front seat of the car with Pa, and Pauline in the back with Nanny. On one occasion, Pa, in the front seat, left to pick up Berlin and Pauline, with Nanny in the back of the car. Or Pa thought that was the case. Actually, when he pulled the car up to the front of the house to leave, he thought Nanny was in the back seat. The truth was that she was chasing after the car yelling, "Pa! Wait! Wait!" Not hearing her, he kept right on driving over to the Bryants. When he arrived, Berlin got into the front seat. He inquired, "Where's Nanny?" Pa rattled off the reply, "She's back there swelled up about something. I been talking to her the whole time and she ain't said a word all the way over here." "Well, there's a good reason for that," Berlin answered, "She's not back there."

I have no idea what Pa must have said, or for that matter, what Nanny must have said when he went back to pick her up. You'll have to use your imagination. But, I know one thing for sure. Pa had to begin the trip all over, and he was probably running late.

Life may seem to be one failed journey after another sometimes. Starting over after failure is never easy. The will to try again when the opportunity is given is at the heart of life. Genesis introduces the God of beginnings and the God of beginning again. God is the God of second chances—and third chances, and fourth chances, and on and on, indefinitely. One can begin afresh today with the God of new beginnings. It is okay to do it. God expects you to.

GENESIS

The story of the Old Testament begins in Genesis. The book opens with the statement, "In the beginning God created the heavens and the earth" (Gen. 1:1). Everything else in the Bible is a continuation of that statement and a commentary upon it.

The Universal Questions (Gen. 1–11): Genesis has two large parts. The first part is found in the first eleven chapters. Genesis 1–11 contains the universal questions all people ask, and the answers the Old Testament gives to those questions. One of the questions is, "Who is responsible for the universe?" The Old Testament answer is, "Yahweh (Jehovah) is responsible. He created it." Another question is, "Who is responsible for the turmoil man finds in his life?" The Old Testament answer is, "Man is. He creates it. He creates it by running away from the God who created him. The created one tries to take the place of his Creator. This is man's mistake, his sin."

Neither God nor man is happy with this situation. Man loses his chance for the good life in the Garden of Eden. And God loses his fellowship with man. As a result, a great flood overwhelms man. But God is the God of second chances. Man is allowed to try again, beginning with Noah, who rode out the flood because of his obedience. In fact, God makes his first covenant with man at this point. The covenant is that he will not wipe out man with a flood again. (It should be said here that one can understand the Old Testament by following the covenant concept through the books.) Noah and his descendants have their ups and downs. They do fairly well. Many are mentioned in a long genealogy.

However, things fall to pieces again in chapter 11. The people build a tower, or ziggurat, to reach into the heavens. Man is pictured trying to climb into the domain of God again, to take his place. Again he fails. This time his language is confused as a result. People can no longer construct the tower. They cannot communicate. Now, what does man do?

A Particular Answer (Gen. 12–50): The answer is found in a second covenant or agreement God makes with man. If the questions are universal ones about life in chapters 1–11, the answer in chapters 12–50 is a particular answer given through a particular people. The focus is narrowed dramatically from chapter 11 to chapter 12. The Old Testament is not a history of man in general. It is the history of a particular people. It is not a history of mankind. It is a history of the people God uses to give an answer to man's predicament in life.

The story of the people of the covenant is actually told through four main characters. They are Abraham, Isaac, Jacob, and Joseph. Through these personalities, God hammers out his covenant. For example, he speaks of the covenant to Abraham in this fashion, "Go from your country and your kindred and your father's house to the land I will show you. I will make you a great nation, and I will bless you, and make your name great, so that you will be a blessing" (12:1–3). It is his intention to nurture these people as they maintain a good working relationship with him. They, in turn, will multiply, become a great people, and become a blessing to mankind. This two-part sketch of Genesis provides the first building block of the Bible. It is the beginning of many beginnings.

"Though I walk in the midst of trouble, thou dost preserve
my life . . . The Lord will fulfill his purpose for me; thy
steadfast love, O Lord, endures for ever."
Psalm 138:7–8

Chapter Two

DEPARTURES AND DELAYS

There were four of us—all ministers. We were on our way to Kansas City for a meeting. It was early Sunday evening. Our plans were to drive a good bit farther, spend the night, and arrive in Kansas City early the next morning. But passing through a little town in Illinois, we decided to attend worship. Stopping at the first church we came to, we joined the congregation in worship. We were warmly received. The worship was nourishing. But, if I were to tell you here that the proceedings were long, I would be telling you an untruth. They were not long. They were very long. I mean very, very long—as in stretched out, taut, and testy long. Not one of us thought about walking out. We had spent too many hours on the other side of the pews to be impolite. We were captives. We were not slaves in Egypt making brick for the Pharaoh, but we were manifestly detained, captives held against our will.

We were in bad shape also. One of us needed to adjourn to the restroom in the worst way. Moreover, two of the party were afflicted with a bad case of the heebie-jeebies, and the fourth was nervously drumming his fingers on the pew in exasperation, thinking none of the little ladies around us could hear him. Obviously, his good judgment had already left him.

Just how bad our condition really was, however, was clarified enormously when the preacher came to that point in his sermon when he solemnly announced, "And finally . . ." We knew then it would be 30 minutes more, at the least. We tried to hang on, and he eventually drained out. We would be saved yet!

Or so we thought. With one us standing cross-legged, two ready to lunge for the door, and the fourth now squeezing his handprints into the back of the oak pew, the song leader announced the closing hymn.

Disaster! The hymn had six verses. We were to sing seven of them! The song leader standing before the congregation was a woman. While patting her high-heeled shoe resoundingly on the hardwood floor, we sang. Would you care to guess the name of the hymn? Give it a try. We sang *I Just Feel like Traveling On*. Can you believe it? *I Just Feel like Traveling On*. All eight verses!

Each of us wanted to approach the little lady and say, "Ma'am, you just think you feel like traveling on. There are four of us who are undone and shriveled up. We are *really* ready to travel on. Let us go!"

And mercifully, they did. At a quarter to ten.

Sometimes there seems to be no exodus in life. We remain in bondage continually. The release eventually found by the slaves in Egypt does not come to us. Where there is no way out, can God make his way in to us? A writer of one of the Psalms reminds us that even if we were to make our home in Hades itself, God would find us. When we cannot get out, we have the option of asking the God of strength and perseverance to come in. Why not ask him?

EXODUS

Perhaps you have seen hay stacked about a pole for cattle to eat. Exodus is the pole around which the Old Testament is stacked. The story of Exodus is the story of a people enslaved in Egypt, probably under the iron fist of Pharaoh Seti I (1308–1290 B.C.). After Yahweh sent a series of plagues against Egypt, the slaves were allowed to leave. Moses was the leader sent to direct their departure. They left about 1290 B.C.

Under the care of Yahweh, they made their way out of Egypt, across the Sea, and into a wilderness in the Midian and Mt. Sinai area. At Sinai they met Yahweh through the leadership of Moses. It was on this mountain that they were brought into a covenant relationship with Yahweh. They were given the Ten Commandments. "Keep these commands and I will be your God," Yahweh promised.

This is the story of the Exodus. It is a story told over and over in the Bible. Sometimes it is retold in the Psalms to remind the people of their past. It is told in families to teach children who they are. And after the captivity in Babylon, it is the background for describing a new exodus.

Exodus, then, is the theme of the Old Testament, the story around which all others are grouped. It should be noted again that the concept of covenant can also be understood as a theme of the Old Testament. At this point, for example, Yahweh is speaking of a covenant for the third time. The first was the covenant made with man after the flood, the second was the covenant made with Abraham, and the third is the covenant made with the giving of the law at Sinai. The covenant idea is bound up with the concept of the Exodus.

Like Genesis, Exodus can be remembered in two parts. The first part (roughly 1–19) is the relating of the event of the Exodus, and the second part, 20–40, is the covenant and its laws. The two parts are joined together with a passage called the "Eagles' Wings" passage (19:3–6).

Finally, you may want to think of the relationship between Genesis and Exodus in this fashion: Exodus is the event that forges the people of the covenant. Genesis is made up of the questions these people have about the world and man (1–11), and the story of their ancestors, the patriarchs (12–50).

"I will sing to the Lord because he has
dealt bountifully with me."
Psalm 13:6

Chapter Three

TO WORSHIP

Susan was giving a demonstration speech in speech class. Her intention was to describe a horse and to indicate the proper way to mount the four-footed beast. She began. "This is the head." She pointed to her right. "This is the tail." She pointed to her left. "This is the saddle here in the middle." She pointed halfway between her right and left. Having thus described the horse, she instructed the class, "And this is how you mount the steed." Climbing upon the demonstration table, and with a measure of fanfare as she readied herself for the task, Susan promptly raised her leg over her imaginary horse and immediately faced the *rear*. This, mind you, on the horse she herself had created and carefully positioned to be properly mounted. The class responded as you might expect.

With respect to worship, the most important thing is not the rules or the description. It is not, "What is it?" It is not even, "How do you do it?" It is losing ourselves in simple adoration of God and quiet meditation in his presence. He usually does the rest.

LEVITICUS

The proper worship for the people of the covenant is defined in the book of Leviticus. The role of the priest is underlined. Aaron and his sons led in the early worship. Leviticus describes those matters related to the priest and worship. Ordination, priestly garments, sacrifice, holy days, holidays, and the laws making up a Holiness Code are all a part of Leviticus. The Holiness Code (17–26) reveals the way the people are to dedicate themselves to the services of God and to their neighbors. A familiar passage is found in the Holiness Code, "You shall love your neighbor as yourself" (19:18).

At this point, we have a book about proper worship—the book of Leviticus. This worship is for people who have emerged from slavery and have pledged themselves to a covenant with Yahweh, including laws—the book of Exodus. These same people have raised questions about man and his universe, while looking back at their ancestors, the patriarchs—the book of Genesis. Such is the relationship of the three books.

> "Do they not err that devise evil? Those who devise good
> meet loyalty and faithfulness."
> Proverbs 14:22

Chapter Four
IS THAT A DONKEY LYING IN YOUR PATH?

There is an unusual story in Numbers 22–24. It is the story of a lowly donkey who is smarter than his rider. The cast of the story includes Balaam, a Mesopotamian prophet. He is joined by Balak, the king of Moab, and a stubborn donkey who Balaam tried to ride.

The three met in this fashion: the people of the covenant are making their way up the King's Highway, east of the Jordan River, when they come to the country of Moab. The King of Moab bars their path. Fighting breaks out between the people of the covenant and the Moabites. Things look bleak for Moab, so Balak the king got in touch with Balaam the prophet to place a curse on the covenant people. Apparently Balaam was not a follower of Yahweh. Archeologists have found his name associated with gods other than the covenant God. So the foreign prophet Balaam is called to place the curse. At this point, there seems to be confusion in the account. Balaam consults Yahweh about the matter at hand. Apparently, Yahweh tells him to take the money Balak has offered and do the job. But then Yahweh gets angry with Balaam for setting out to do the very thing he seems to have told him to do. Balaam meets with Balak a second time. This time it appears acceptable to all parties for him to place the curse. He sets out to do it.

The account seems contradictory. Was it all right with Yahweh or not? Probably it was not right with Yahweh either time. The account can be understood by remembering the principle of "first cause." As a means of understanding the Old Testament, first cause refers to the practice of describing an event without considering the action of secondary parties. In other words, God is thought of as having caused all things directly. From that perspective, I would say, "Going through the swamp, God stubbed my big toe against a log." From the opposite perspective, I would say, "I stubbed my toe." For the Hebrew writer, God is the first cause of all things. Shifting the account to the secondary party, the writer might have said something like the following: Balaam was offered money to curse the people. It was not enough, so he didn't go. He was offered more money the second time, and he went to curse the invading people of the covenant.

The story gets interesting at this point. Balaam gets on a donkey to go do the job he has been paid to do. But on the way, the donkey carries him off the road into a field. Next he scrapes the prophet's leg as he pushes him into a stone wall, and finally he lies down in the middle of the road, refusing to go any farther. Climbing off the animal to deal with the situation, Balaam is startled. The donkey speaks to him, highly offended. He tells Balaam that he has no right to treat him so shabbily. The donkey has always tried to treat Balaam fairly. In this particular instance, the donkey, knowing that the messenger of God stood in Balaam's way to block his mission, was doing his rider a favor by lying down, refusing to go farther. In the give and take of their conversation, the donkey gets the better of the exchange. The one being ridden is smarter than the one riding. Whether you think that the donkey is verbalizing or that Balaam understands the message non-verbally, the communication is the same. Balaam needs to cancel his mission. But continuing on his way, each attempt Balaam makes to place a curse on the people turns into a blessing instead. Yahweh has seen to that. It is no wonder, then, that King Balak cancels Balaam's contract and sends him away.

What an unusual story—a tough one to apply. We live in a mean world. Sometimes it seems to get meaner by the day. In a mean world, getting slammed around means cursing back. It means ill will, not goodwill. It means to hold grudges. It means to pay back.

Rocked back upon ours heels by life, it seems wrong to pray for our enemies or to do good to those who mistreat us. It seems "donkeyfied" at best. It seems there is no way that a donkey is going to have the last say in a mean-spirited world. The truth of the matter is that he may. Goodwill may reduce stress a little. It may positively affect internal well-being a little. It may help lower blood pressure a little. It may provide a chance for better heart action. It may produce a fuller life. In such instances, speaking like a donkey may be considered a blessing. And that is considering only the physical effects of the matter, not to mention the spiritual or mental. This being the case, perhaps more donkeys ought to be allowed to speak.

Is that a donkey lying down in your path?

NUMBERS

The book of Numbers continues the journey the people made out of Egypt and through the wilderness to the southern border of Canaan. Canaan, or Palestine, as it was called later, is the land they will claim in the name of their covenant God, Yahweh.

However, the initial entry from the south is not successful, and they are forced to remain in the wilderness for another generation. They will eventually march around the tip of the Dead Sea, up the King's Highway, and successfully enter into the land from the east.

Complaining against their leader, Moses, marks this stage of the people's journey. They complain about a lack of food and about Moses' marriage to a foreign wife. A rebellion is even mounted against Moses by a trio led by Korah. It is put down. During this period, Moses' brother, Aaron, and his sister, Miriam, die. Moses himself gets angry while striking a prescribed rock to produce a flow of water for the people. As a result, he is doomed to die without entering the land of promise.

It is probably enough to see this fourth book simply as the continuation of the journey to Canaan.

> "The Lord answer you in the day of trouble! The name of the God of Jacob protect you! May he send you help from the sanctuary and give you support from Zion."
> Psalm 20:1–2

Chapter Five

IS GOD OUT TO GET YOU?

Is God out to get you? Before addressing that question, there is a prior question we should honor: "Did God try to kill Moses?" In this last chapter of the Pentateuch (Deut. 34), Moses' death and burial is recorded. But much earlier, on his way to Egypt to ask that the slaves be released, Moses and his family stopped at a lodging place on the way. Here, in the unusual passage found in Exodus 4:24–26, we are told that "the Lord met him and sought to kill him." That is strange because God is the one who asked Moses to go to Egypt in the first place. Why should he kill him? And it is strange that he "sought" to kill him. You would guess that God did not have to seek to kill him. God could simply do it.

In light of the concerns just mentioned, interpreters suggest understanding this as the language of first cause in these verses. God is the cause of everything, so the writer does not bother with secondary causes. If he had, he would probably have said that on the way to Egypt, Moses became deathly ill. His wife, realizing that he had never been circumcised, undertook to remedy the matter. Since Moses was too ill to withstand the procedure, she instead circumcised her son with a flint rock and touched Moses' sexual organ with the removed foreskin in an act of proxy circumcision. (The translators probably used the phrase "Moses' feet" as a euphemism for the real organ.) Zipporah thought that the proxy circumcision would promote Moses' healing, and in some fashion, make him a proper "bridegroom." After this encounter with serious illness, Moses recovered and proceeded to carry out his mission. The conclusion of the matter is that God was not out to get Moses. He did not try to kill him.

Life can become overwhelmingly difficult, dark, and painful. Loss, failure, and disappointment can rob living of any real meaning. It is no wonder that many of us may have shared the feeling from time to time that life may be "out to get us." Looking at the experience of Moses at the lodging place, in spite of not understanding his hurt, can we conclude that God is trying to assist us in the difficult, the dark, the painful, the loss, the failure, and the disappointment? Certainly he is not out to get us, but to instead help us in the face of life's inevitable experiences. A writer of the statement, "God does not willingly afflict or grieve the sons of men," (Lam. 3:33) was saying something similar to that. The writer of the Psalms was concluding something akin to it when he wrote, "God is our refuge and strength, a very present help in trouble" (Ps. 46:1). Life is hard, but God is out to help us.

In your present pain, may you be able to find the help of God and continue on your way refreshed.

DEUTERONOMY

Deuteronomy means "second law" in Greek. The title immediately introduces the reader to the development that has taken place. In Exodus, the people of the covenant received the Ten Commandments. As the years passed, the people were faced with continually changing life situations in regard to the law. Take, for example, the law, "Thou shalt not kill." The question arose, "If one planned a murder before committing it, should it make a difference in sentencing the murderer?" By the same token, "If one got into an argument with another, and in the heat of the moment, one man killed the other, should a lack of premeditation make a difference in sentencing the murderer?" These questions, along with innumerable variations of multiple situations as life changed, made for a growth in the law codes. Thus, Deuteronomy—the second law—developed.

In our overview, there are now five books. They make up the first of the great building blocks of the Bible called the Pentateuch, the Torah, or simply the Law. Pulling these five together, the reader has the story of the people leaving Egypt and becoming a covenant people when they received the law at Mt. Sinai (Exodus), the questions these people ask about life and the universe (Gen. 1–11), the stories of their ancestors (Gen. 12–50), the proper worship for the people of the covenant (Leviticus), the continuation of the journey from Egypt to the tip of Palestine (Numbers), and the second law (Deuteronomy).

> "A soft answer turns away wrath,
> but a harsh word stirs up anger."
> Proverbs 15:1

Chapter Six

AIMING HIGH

His mother told him not to hit people—never to fight. He came home in tears, more often than not. Holy war was not suggested to him as a way of dealing with the matter. The battle cry of Deuteronomy was never offered to him. It was a confusing and difficult time, and not easily resolved.

War seems bad in its entirety. How does God feel about it? Perhaps war represents the best that man can do at the moment in the name of freedom and liberty. But I don't believe it represents God's intentions for man. Remember the one called the Prince of Peace, who suggested that when one is struck on one cheek, he or she is to "turn the other," presumably to be struck on that cheek as well. "Blessed are the peacemakers," Jesus said, and, "Do unto others as you would have them do unto you."

But there are always the childhood battles and situations that continue to crop up again and again through life. Therefore, we must try over and over to do better. We may never fully reach the intention of God for man, but we can hope to constantly keep the objective in sight.

JOSHUA

Joshua is the story of the invasion of Canaan by the people of the covenant. On Moses' death, Joshua replaces him as leader, and it is Joshua who leads the people in the subduing of the land. The watchword of the invasion is found in Deuteronomy 20:16–18, given just before the invasion began. It read, "But in the cities of these peoples that the Lord your God gives you for an inheritance, you shall save alive nothing that breathes, but you shall utterly destroy them . . . as the Lord your God has commanded; that they may not teach you to do according to all their abominable practices which they have done in the service of their gods, and so to sin against the Lord your God."

After the capture of many cities, the book features a great reaffirmation of the covenant. Thus, the people who began in slavery and became the people of the covenant at Sinai are now the people who begin settling the land God promised. In reaffirming the covenant, it is once again clear that the story of the Old Testament is the story of Exodus and covenant.

> "Hear my son, your father's instruction, and reject not your mother's teaching, for they are a fair garland for your head and pendants for your neck."
> Proverbs 1:8–9

Chapter Seven
AVOIDING DARK AGES

Simply forgetting to worship God, when prolonged over an extended period, can lead to a "Dark Age" of the spirit.

An idea that stayed with the people of the covenant since the time of Deuteronomy was the call to worship at a single place. It is found in various passages, including Deuteronomy 12:5, "But you shall seek the place which the Lord your God will choose out of all your tribes to put his name and make his habitation there; thither you shall go, and thither you shall bring your burnt offerings and your sacrifices. . . ." The single place probably referred originally to Shiloh or Shechem, both of which seemed to have been major centers of worship. The reaffirmation of the covenant in the book of Joshua took place at Shechem. Many years later, the single place was taken to mean Jerusalem and the temple there.

After the Temple was destroyed in 70 A.D., never to be rebuilt, an interesting emphasis seems to emerge. Now there can be multiple places. Wherever ten men were gathered, they could organize a lay synagogue for worship. The emphasis seems to be upon worship itself and not upon a single place of worship.

Today, our emphasis may be upon a single place of worship, rather than on our effort to remember to worship. My friend Stu Phillips told this little story: a small town had two rather large, imposing church structures. They faced each other on opposite corners across the street. A stranger, puzzled that two large structures would be needed in a small town, asked a local man about the matter. The man summed the matter up quickly, "Oh, the folks in the church on this side think there ain't no hell. And the folks in the church on the other side say, 'The hell there ain't.'" Obviously, each one offered a single place to worship.

Sometimes it is even within the one place itself that the emphasis upon correctness or tradition of worship is emphasized. In a single synagogue, folks on one side said it was the tradition to stand up to say the Shema, their watchword of worship. Folks on the other side of the synagogue said it was the tradition to sit down to say the Shema. Each group made loud noises at the other as each tried to worship. The situation became so bad that a group went to a very wise teacher and asked, "Is the tradition to stand while reciting the Shema?" "No," he answered, "It is not the tradition to stand while reciting the Shema." "Well," the group continued, "Is it the tradition to sit while reciting the Shema?" "No," he replied, "It is not the tradition to sit while reciting the Shema." "But teacher," the group complained, "Our folks make fun of each other. They call each other names back and forth while reciting the Shema." At that point the teacher quickly interrupted with this climactic revelation. "That!" he said, "That problem is the tradition."

Unfortunately! It may be that we get so involved in laying claims to a distinctive place or tradition that an emphasis upon worship itself falls by the wayside. Don't be sidetracked. The best way to avoid a Dark Age of the spirit is to remember, above all, to worship freely and fully.

JUDGES

The period of the Judges ran from about 1200–1020 B.C. Remember that the Exodus occurred about 1290 B.C. and the invasion of Canaan about 1250 B.C.

The Judges were charismatic leaders. They bore resemblances to army generals. They were also a bit like decision-rendering judges. The tribes of the covenant people faced enemies at various places in Canaan. The Judges arose as the enemies arose. As the enemies were defeated, the Judges passed from the scene as well. They held no long-term position. There were many crises, and thus many leaders that came and went during the period.

The period is known as the Dark Ages in the Old Testament. There is a passage early in the book which explains why this is the case. It reads, "And there arose another generation ... who did not know the Lord or the work which he had done for Israel" (2:10). They forgot the Exodus and the covenant. They had come full circle from slavery in Egypt to almost two hundred years in which most of them forgot their heritage under Yahweh.

Among the Judges, there was a powerful woman named Deborah and a wild-hair gambler named Samson.

Our overview now includes a multi-year invasion of Canaan (Joshua) and a two hundred year period of the Dark Ages (Judges). In your mind, add the picture of the first five books of the Old Testament as a preface to Joshua and Judges. This will provide our overview to this point.

"Do not trust in those deceptive words: 'This is the temple of
the Lord, the temple of the Lord, the temple of the Lord.'"
Jeremiah 7:4

Chapter Eight

THE ARK AND FOUR-LEAF CLOVERS

Have you ever looked for four-leaf clovers? They are supposed to mean "good luck" when you discover one, or so I've been told. I've never had much luck finding them.

It's hard to imagine looking at the ark of the covenant as a good luck piece. The ark, forty-five inches long, twenty-seven inches wide, and twenty-seven inches high, was overlaid with gold. It had a mercy seat on top and winged creatures on either end. The seat represented the throne of God. It was carried by two poles that were threaded through rings on the corners of the box. The ark symbolized the presence of God. It was thought to be especially helpful when carried with the people as they fought their enemies. For example, it preceded the people as they crossed the Jordan with Joshua to fight the Canaanites.

In religion, sometimes we transfer our faith from the reality a thing symbolizes to faith in the thing itself. The thing then becomes a four-leaf clover. This happened to the ark as the people carried it into battle with the Philistines. They lost the battle. Even the ark was captured (1 Sam. 4:10–22).

This is an old observation. Many have observed it. Have you ever noticed that the folks who have the most good luck are the ones who work the hardest? Faith was never meant to be translated into good luck. Good luck fades and life falls apart. When life falls apart, our best chance for strength and encouragement is in a faith that keeps on keeping on. Today may be a good day to keep on keeping on. May you be bountifully rewarded by doing that!

1 AND 2 SAMUEL

Samuel, in scroll form, was long enough that it found its way into two parts in book form. Thus we have a continuous story but two books.

Picking up our story at the end of Judges, we understand that the nearly two hundred years of the Dark Ages had been an extremely difficult time for the people of the Exodus. They had tried to function as a loosely joined confederacy of tribes. Continual battles with their enemies took a toll. To improve their chances against attacking enemies, two modes of government were suggested. The first was to continue as they had been, which invited disaster. The second was to choose a king and become a monarchy. The second choice won, although that choice was debated for many years afterward, especially after the great king David died.

The monarchy emerged with Saul, a sort of judge-king figure who bridged the gap from the confederacy to the monarchy. Then came the great soldier, poet, statesman, and king, David. Finally came Solomon, who marked the beginning of the downfall of the monarchy. At his death, the monarchy split into two parts.

1 and 2 Samuel tell the story of the beginning of the monarchy.

> "And behold, the Lord passed by, and a great and strong wind rent the mountains, and broke in pieces the rocks before the Lord, but the Lord was not in the wind; and after the wind, an earthquake, but the Lord was not [there]; and after the earthquake, a fire, but the Lord was not [there], and after the fire, a still small voice, and [therein] Elijah heard [God]."
> 1 Kings 19:11–13

Chapter Nine

WORSHIP IN A GIANT INSECT-EXPLODING WORLD

Long before my friend Grover Covington became a judge, and even before he was asked to play a charity high school basketball game in his BVDs, he worked part-time at Newman's Department Store. It must have been a bad day for him as a salesman. I remember it was a bad day for me. My mama had dragged me into the store to buy a shirt or something or other. I was unhappy, as young kids are apt to be under such circumstances. Shuffling my feet while drumming my fingers on the counter, I mumbled something continually under my breath. I alternately bumped and thumped my head and back end against the wall. You get the picture. Grover did. And it was too much for him on a bad day. "Can't you be still?" he asked in his best salesman-in-control manner. Well, he sorta caught me off guard, because I didn't expect him to ask me that particular question. As it turned out, Mama bought the shirt about that time, and I didn't have to answer.

To tell you the truth, I couldn't be still. I think I had Attention Deficit Hyperactivity Disorder before they knew what to call it. Sometimes I think I still have it. And between that and seeing too many movie previews in which giant alien insects—and every available automobile, truck, ship, train, plane, skyscraper, and all in between—are blown to smithereens, I was ready to bounce off the wall.

It is through such obstacles that we are called to worship.

In 1 Kings 18–19, the prophet Elijah had given Jezebel and her priests a powerful rebuff, but then he ran away into the wilderness with Jezebel howling on his heels. He looked for God, but in his harried state of mind, he only found noise. He found the wind. He found the earthquake. He found the lightning and fire. God spared him the exploding giant insects.

Elijah was looking in the wrong way, in the wrong places. It was when he sat down and quietly waited that the still small voice of God emerged to speak to Elijah's bouncing and besieged being!

Would you like to try it now for a minute? Two minutes? Three? If you don't mind, I'll wait with you (I wish I could have done that for Grover). Peace.

1 AND 2 KINGS

The picture in 1 and 2 Kings is that of Solomon and the beginning of the end of the monarchy. Solomon's taxation and harsh policies led to the dividing of the monarch.

Two parts of the monarchy resulted. The northern portion was called Israel. It lasted from 922 to 722–21 B.C. Judah, the southern part, lasted longer. It continued until 587–86 B.C. At that time, the people were taken into exile in Babylon.

Recall that our overview began with the exodus out of Egyptian slavery. The people became the people of the covenant at Sinai with the receiving of the law (Exodus). The questions the people ask about the universe and man are found in Genesis 1–11, with the story of their ancestors, the patriarchs, in Genesis 12–50. Leviticus tells of proper worship. Numbers relates the continued journey toward the promised land, and Deuteronomy pictures the second law. Joshua continues the story with the conquest of the promised land. Judges tells of the nearly two hundred year period when the people forgot their heritage. 1 and 2 Samuel introduce the monarchy, and 1 and 2 Kings introduce the divided kingdom.

"Fill me with joy and gladness; let the bones thou hast broken rejoice. Hide thy face from my sins, and blot out all my iniquities."
Psalm 51:8

Chapter Ten

A 3x5 GLOSSY WITH NO FLAWS, PLEASE

If you are like many people, you have looked at a snapshot of yourself and said, "That's a bad picture," or "That doesn't look like me." You may have even torn the offending picture from an album and tossed it into a wastebasket. You may have wished for a picture that minimized your flaws, as in a "David without Bathsheba" story.

I had one such picture. It was done by a charcoal artist. There was one thing wrong with it. It didn't look like me. It looked like Franklin Delano Roosevelt Jr. (All of the artist's male portraits resembled FDR Jr. All of his female portraits resembled Jane Wyman). Of course, the drawing didn't reveal any flaws, either. It is in the attic now. It is not much good, unless you are FDR Jr.

If you have been around for awhile, life has provided its share of bumps, breaks, cuts, scars, and bruises, inside and out, physical and emotional. It might be nice to have a picture without any of these flaws. But such a picture would not be of us, of course.

Lest we forget, the storms of life have been known to produce strong, weathered faces and folks of appealing character. Beloved. Unique. Irreplaceable, for all who know them. Priceless pictures that cannot be duplicated.

The flaws within? They are vivid reminders of our humanity. But they can be turned over to a flawless God who will wipe them out. That opportunity should be hard to resist!

Still want a 3x5 glossy with no flaws? What about your baby pictures!

1 AND 2 CHRONICLES

These books tell the same story of the monarchy and divided kingdom that is told in 1 and 2 Samuel and 1 and 2 Kings. Some of the passages are identical to those in the first accounts. Passages about King David and other kings of Judah, however, sometimes pay little attention to the weaknesses of these kings. For example, the David and Bathsheba story is omitted in Chronicles. It is thought that Chronicles was written later than the other accounts, perhaps a good bit later than the Babylonian Exile.

1 and 2 Chronicles repeat but do not appreciably move forward the story of the people of the covenant. Some of their spokesmen or prophets do that in the next chapters.

> "But thou art near O Lord, and all thy commandments are true."
> Psalm 119:151

Chapter Eleven

IF IT HAD BEEN A SNAKE

"If it had been a snake, it would have bitten you." Those were often the words spoken to me by my father when I failed to see close at hand the very thing I had been looking for.

It is true that in the prosperous world of Amos's day, the nation did ignore and violate the covenant. And this spelled national disaster for the covenant people. But at the same time, it meant something else. An opportunity was close at hand to take a giant step forward in their faith. While Amos was calling them up to the level of their covenant religion, God was close at hand, trying to pull their understanding up even higher, beyond where they had ever been. If that understanding had been a snake, the snake would have bitten them. The problem was that they had always thought God was theirs alone. But in Amos 9:5–6, there is an enormous idea, namely that God is the God of all nations. He had even provided an exodus for the Philistines and an exodus for the Syrians. (That is an interesting turn on the concept of the Exodus, is it not?) But they were not quite ready for that idea. Perhaps the biggest sin in all of Amos is that the covenant people were nowhere near as developed in their religious understanding as God intended. This affected the scope of their ethical failure.

In our world, perhaps patience is needed, or acceptance is needed, or forgiveness is needed, or there is some other gem

God wants to give to us, but we're frantically busy with ourselves and don't recognize its presence. If it were a snake, it would bite us. God won't bite. But he is close at hand, anxious to pull us forward into the very understanding we most need. The real disaster in our busy lives is the failure to slow down enough to accept what God has to give us. Today, in the turmoil of all our busyness, maybe we are to quietly stretch out our hands in faith to ask for the gift that is closer than we think. Make the effort. It may be the beginning of a giant step forward in your faith understanding.

AMOS

Amos, a shepherd, was one of several spokesmen for God. They were called prophets. They spoke during the period just before the fall of the northern kingdom (750 B.C.) to just after Judah's return from exile (500 B.C.). Their words, spoken in short, pointed sayings (oracles), were meant to be heard. Disciples memorized them, and they were later written down in the books of the prophets. They were not so much predictors of the future as they were proclaimers of God's message to that day. Their popularity was not great during their lifetimes. However, later generations recognized the truth of their sayings.

Amos viewed Israel about three decades before she fell to the Assyrians. He recognized that the end was near. His recognition was tied to Israel's failure to keep the covenant. He saw ethical failure. Judges received bribes in the courtroom. Merchants placed heavy thumbs on their scales to cheat the customer in the marketplace. Crowds attended worship but without sincerity or depth of meaning. Wealth was abused. The poor were mistreated. Amos described these and other violations of the covenant. Recognizing Israel's failures and seeing the shadow of mighty Assyria hanging like a dark cloud overhead, Amos could see disaster ahead for his people. It occurred in 722–21 B.C.

If the Pentateuch introduces us to the people of the covenant, Joshua takes us into the promised land with them. Then Judges exposes us to the two hundred year period of their

Dark Ages, while 1 and 2 Samuel, 1 and 2 Kings, and 1 and 2 Chronicles take us through the experience of the monarchy and the divided kingdoms to their demise. Beginning with Amos, the prophets address the many issues of concern as they witness the ups and downs of the people in relation to the covenant.

"And the Lord said to me, 'Go again, love a woman who is beloved of a paramour and is an adulteress; even as the Lord loves the people of Israel, though they turn to other gods and love cakes of raisins.'"
Hosea 3:1

Chapter Twelve

Unexpected Developments

Stu Phillips, whom I quoted earlier, told the story of a couple about to be married. The bride-to-be came from an affluent family. The groom's family was not well off. But the mother of the groom wanted to do something special that the couple would always remember. She offered to supply the wedding cake for the reception. It was agreed that she do so.

The mother knew that the couple might be anxious about the outset of their marriage, as some couples are. She wanted them to feel at ease and confident. Therefore, she chose a passage from the New Testament book of 1 John to help them. It was 1 John 4:18: "There is no fear in love, but perfect love casts out fear." She asked the baker to scroll the passage on the cake for the couple to see. He followed directions well, with one exception. He thought the passage was from John 4:18 and placed that passage on the cake.

The couple and the families saw the cake for the first time at the reception. The cake had the words of John 4:18 written on it: ". . . you have had five husbands, and he whom you now have is not your husband. . . ."

No doubt the unexpected words did not have the desired effect the groom's mother had hoped for.

In misunderstandings, we can sometimes see the storm clouds gathering, as Hosea saw them gathering over Israel. We can try to make preparation for coming trouble. At other times, the trouble comes quickly and unexpectedly. Most of us seek equilibrium in life. But try as we may, the equilibrium seems to escape us time and again. Misunderstandings happen. There is a constant that can be applied, however. Not being able to control external factors, expected or unexpected, we can hope for the best for the other party in a relationship. That is, love is the constant that can eventually right the relationship if it is applied. As long as one party holds to this constant, there is the possibility for equilibrium again.

It takes two to tango, but someone has to ask the other to dance. Love them. Ask. I believe that is what Hosea is saying.

HOSEA

Writing just before the fall of Israel, Hosea witnessed the floundering disintegration of the northern kingdom. It was difficult for him to watch. Hosea acknowledged the weaknesses of the covenant people, but he still loved them.

His book essentially says that though the people disappointed God, God continued to love them. Hosea conveyed this understanding in a special way. He pictures a husband (himself!) whose wife is unfaithful. Although the unfaithful wife plays the harlot, God counsels the husband to take her back. In receiving her, Hosea tells the reader that this is the way God feels toward his people. Though they have prostituted their faith, he loves them nevertheless. In picturing the nature of God in this fashion, some students of the Old Testament understand that Hosea stands closest of all Old Testament books to the New Testament understanding of God.

A second spokesman has now assessed the condition of the people of the covenant. Amos described ethical failure. Hosea has seen failure but is certain of the unceasing love of God.

"In peace I will both lie down and sleep; for thou alone,
O Lord, makest me dwell in safety."
Psalm 4:8

Chapter Thirteen

IN QUIETNESS AND CONFIDENCE

Problems, like rabbits, seem to multiply rapidly. We think we have enough only to have other problems surface out of nowhere. Awhile ago, there was the Y2K computer problem. Children, some of whom seem to appear on any scene with a certain calmness, were of help. A first grade teacher I know was trying to drum up interest in the year 2000. "Does anyone know what is going to happen in the year 2000?" she asked her class. One youngster whose juices were flowing replied, "Yes, everybody who bought furniture from Rooms-to-Go is going to have to pay their bill!"

The first grader didn't know it, or maybe he did, but in facing problems, humor helps. However, Isaiah counsels a quiet, confident faith as an additional method. He reminds us, "In returning and rest you shall be saved; in quietness and trust shall be your strength" (Isa. 30:15).

The quietness itself is helpful. But in the quietness, trust can come up with sought-for answers to nagging problems. It wouldn't hurt to multiply our quiet time.

ISAIAH

Isaiah of Jerusalem is a third voice speaking for God in the eighth century B.C. Amos and Hosea spoke to the northern kingdom. Isaiah speaks to the southern kingdom. He addresses issues of the covenant also. Of course, Judah doesn't fall until a century and a half later in 587–86 B.C.

Isaiah is concerned with the holiness of the covenant people. That is, he counsels them to respond to a moral God with moral living. At the same time, he urges them to exercise a quiet and confident faith in God. Military crises in the nation should inspire the people to trust in God. Moreover, even though destruction of the nation comes about, Isaiah understands it to be a refining process. Out of that refining process, a remnant of covenant people will emerge. They will start the covenant community anew. An echo of the Exodus can be heard here. In starting anew, the people would be led by the Messiah, the ideal David.

> "For thy steadfast love is before my eyes, and I
> walk in faithfulness to thee."
> Psalm 26:3

Chapter Fourteen

THE IMPORTANCE OF VERBS

"The way you live speaks so loudly, I cannot hear what you are saying." In this well-known statement, the emphasis is upon being a person of integrity. It takes precedence over talking about integrity or talking about religion. In summing up the understanding of the prophets, Micah made a similar statement. Notice the emphasis he places on verbs. It is important for a person of the covenant to *do*—to "do justice." It is important to *love*—"to love kindness." It is important to *walk*—"to walk humbly with God."

In this communication age, there is an overwhelming amount of talking. There is almost constant dialog about religion taking place on television, radio, the internet, and elsewhere daily. To our age, Micah would promote "the walk" over "the talk." There is nothing wrong with talk as such, of course. But the best talk is to walk one's faith. And this is a good thing. Many of us feel that we cannot talk well. The beautiful thing is that we can all walk well by daily living out our faith. We can all engage in what is most important.

MICAH

The fourth figure in a quartet of spokesmen or prophets was Micah. He spoke before the northern kingdom fell, directing part of his message to the north.

Micah summed up for us the essential message of the eighth century prophets. He wrote in a famous passage, "He has showed you, O man, what is good; and what does the Lord require of you but to do justice, and to love kindness, and to walk humbly with our God" (6:8).

Speaking of the covenant, he underscores Amos's theme (justice), Hosea's theme (love or kindness), and Isaiah's theme (a quiet, confident walk with God). In this fashion, the prophets addressed issues in the lives of the covenant people.

At this point we have come nearly half way through the Old Testament. Our overview should include ten parts:

1. The Exodus (Exodus)
2. Universal questions (Gen. 1–11)
3. Ancestors of the people (Gen. 12–50)
4. Proper worship (Leviticus)
5. Journey of people continued (Numbers)
6. Second Law (Deuteronomy)
7. Conquest of Canaan (Joshua)
8. Dark Ages (Judges)
9. Monarchy and divided kingdom (1 and 2 Samuel, 1 and 2 Kings, and 1 and 2 Chronicles)
10. Prophets and issues (Amos, Hosea, Isaiah, and Micah)

We are reminded that the Old Testament is an historical religion. It does not take place in space or in a vacuum. It occurs during time and on the plane of history. Think of the Old Testament as a train moving through history. As it rolls, it unfolds the story of the people of the covenant. The engine that powers it is the Exodus. It is coupled with the reflection on universal questions and ancestors. These first two units are connected to seven that follow, each bearing one segment of the story.

> "And I said to her, 'You must dwell as mine for many days; you shall not play the harlot, or belong to another man. So will I also be to you.'"
> Hosea 3:3

Chapter Fifteen
OVER MARRIAGE'S THRESHOLDS

A reference is made to an unusual custom in Zephaniah 1:7–9. Although not a custom of the covenant people, some practiced it. The prophet reprimanded them. The custom was referred to as "leaping over the threshold." A demon was thought to live there, and to step on the threshold would produce evil. Today's custom of carrying the bride over the threshold probably came from a similar belief.

Obviously, along with Zephaniah, folks now deny the existence of a threshold demon and understand why he despised the foreign custom. At the same time, we are aware of the great number of "demons" or problems modern marriages face. Therefore, something good might be said for today's custom.

There are not many demons of marriage that could not be exorcised if the couple were willing to "carry" each other over demonic thresholds. Of course, to be effective, the willingness to do so needs to continue after the honeymoon—especially after the honeymoon. Is there a demon hanging around the threshold in your marriage? Perhaps the solution is to "carry" your beloved over the threshold. He/she is not heavy. After all he/she is your mate.

ZEPHANIAH

The "day of the Lord" is the theme of Zephaniah. Writing about fifty years before Judah fell, he listed worship of idols, worship of heavenly bodies, and similar worship, contrary to the worship of the covenant God, as shortcomings of the people. He added that Judah's leaders had led her astray. Even some of her prophets were immoral.

In light of this, the coming day of the Lord would be a day of darkness and judgment. However, like the other prophets, he didn't leave the matter there. His was a message of hope as well. A better day was coming (3:8–13). Jerusalem would be restored (3:14–20).

"For as he thinketh in his heart, so is he. . . ."
Proverbs 23:7

Chapter Sixteen

Straightening Leaning Towers

Nahum had strong feelings about Assyria. The nation had abused and misused his people. These feelings must have risen to the surface quickly when he wrote about the fall of Nineveh in about 612 B.C. We can understand. He was not writing from the perspective of Jesus or even Hosea.

Some of the time, life can be affected and even changed by the perspective we take toward it. For a long time now, I have travelled south on I-65 between Nashville and Franklin, Tennessee. I have never failed to be impressed by a tall radio tower standing on the left side of the interstate. Approaching it, while climbing a high, curved incline, it is apparent that the tower is leaning. It seems to be off center by ten or fifteen degrees. Yet it is tied down by long cables that hold it securely in place. A well-grounded, but leaning tower! The first time I saw it, I wondered how the builders could have allowed it to happen. However, an interesting thing happens as a driver moves through the high curved incline and begins to make his way into the decline. Looking at the tower, while approaching level road once again, it is clear that the radio tower is perfectly straight. It is not leaning at all. The only problem with the picture is the driver's perspective. From my point of view on the high curved incline, I thought the tower was leaning. But from my perspective on level ground, it was straight.

Life can appear to be leaning and off center. However, the problem may not be in the situation we face, but in our perspective of it. "No one really cares." "All the really good men have passed away." "They don't make people like they used to." "You can't trust anyone anymore."

That may be. But maybe we should take another look. The problem may be in our perspective. At least this was true of one of the prophets we have been considering. Elijah was feeling sorry for himself after having run away from Jezebel. Sitting in the wilderness, God asked him, "What are you doing here, Elijah?" Elijah answered that he was the only faithful servant of the Lord left. Just how distorted his perspective was became clear when God directed him to "Get up and get busy." The true picture is that there were seven thousand people in Israel who were still faithful (1 Kings 19:9–18).

The handy thing about a wrong perspective is that it can be changed. When it is changed, life usually straightens up. Maybe we ought to take a look at some old perspectives. Perhaps it would even be helpful to look at the ones listed above. There may be a warped one in there we would like to exchange for a new one. The exchange might make a difference in our outlook on life.

NAHUM

Nahum is consumed with the fall of Nineveh. Nineveh was the capital of Assyria, the nation that conquered the northern kingdom in 722–21 B.C. A little over a hundred years later, Nineveh itself fell. It was destroyed jointly by the Medes and Babylonians. Nahum, the prophet, wrote about it in an acrostic poem. He used the different letters of the alphabet to begin each line of his writing.

The poem celebrated the fall of Nineveh at the hands of an avenging God. It was not simple vengeance, however. Nahum's picture was that of God as the God of justice.

> "O Lord . . . why dost thou make me see
> wrongs and look upon trouble?"
> Habakkuk 1:2–3

Chapter Seventeen

WHY DID YOU DO THAT, GOD?

Some of us grew up under the parental slogan, "Children are meant to be seen and not heard." Obedience was an expectation, not self-expression. A similar environment must have been found among the people of the covenant prior to Habakkuk. Just as the pendulum swung from silence to self-expression in our society, so in Judah it seems to have moved slightly in that direction with Habakkuk.

Is it okay to question? Habakkuk and some of the voices of the later Judean experience answer in the positive. Sometimes, it seems almost necessary. It clears the channel of communication between God and man. Afterwards, God can speak again. The bereaved person may be angry with God. Perhaps he or she blames God for the suffering a loved one went through before dying. In this case, expressing one's anger with God may be the key to opening the floodgates of grief. The healing may begin. Questioning God is not unfaithfulness. It can be the opening of faith's door to help and understanding.

HABAKKUK

Among the prophets, Habakkuk raises a different voice. He is the questioning prophet. He asks God why he does certain acts.

Habakkuk's predecessors had declared what God was doing. He wants to know why God was doing it. Recognizing this departure from his contemporaries, some refer to Habakkuk as the philosopher-prophet.

An example of his questioning is in 1:1–4 where he asks, "Lord how long must this flaunting of your will go on?" It seems that Judah is flaunting the will of God only a few years before the Babylonians are going to conquer the nation. Habakkuk wants to know why God allows this. God's answer is that the Chaldeans (Babylonians) are going to punish Judah for her disobedience. This prompted Habakkuk's second question, "Lord, how can you punish us with people who are more unrighteous that we are?" (1:12–17) The answer was slow in coming. Climbing a watchtower to wait, Habakkuk finally received God's answer: God did things by his own timetable. Moreover, people faithful to the Lord would survive. He sums up the matter in these words, "The righteous shall live by faith" (2:4).

> "Blessed are all who take refuge in him."
> Psalm 2:12

Chapter Eighteen
IN THE PALM OF HIS HAND

We are familiar with the Rock of Gibraltar or a pair of cupped hands as symbols of security. For the people of Judah, it was the Temple. In his Temple Sermon (7:1–15; 26:1–14), Jeremiah aroused the anger of the people. He insisted that the people were trusting in the Temple rather than in their covenant relationship with God. Much like their ancestors who trusted in the Ark of the Covenant, they saw "magic" in the Temple. It was seen as their protection, their security. They thought that God would not let anything happen to Jerusalem because the Temple was there. They believed he would not let anything happen to the Temple because it was his house. They were wrong on both counts.

A neighbor in his twenties worked installing window framing on a multi-story hotel that was under construction. His work entailed crawling outside the windows onto a scaffold. Introducing a helper to the work, he reportedly anchored his scaffold inside the construction using concrete blocks. It was said to have been set up in a rather unorthodox manner. Crawling out the window, twenty stories or so up, he and his helper fell to their deaths. The concrete anchors had shifted under their weight.

Commenting on the tragedy, the man's father explained that his son's new found faith caused him to believe nothing bad would happen to him. But, tragically, that supposed security failed him.

Our security is not that we are kept from having bad things happen to us. Rather, our security is that God is with us when they do happen. He "who was tempted in every way even as we are," is by our side. We are not forsaken. He is there for us.

The faith of the covenant people may not have prevented the fall of Jerusalem any more than a "magic" Temple did. However, faith would have enabled them to accept the tragedy when it occurred. It would have empowered them within, to overcome their captivity.

JEREMIAH

Jeremiah the prophet was on the scene as Judah went into sharp decline. He tried unsuccessfully to prevent the fall. While taking his message to Jehoiakin and other rulers, he was simultaneously pointing out the shortcomings of Judah. He saw judgment coming. His work was to no avail as Judah fell to the Babylonians in 587–86 B.C.

While in and out of jail at the hands of his enemies, his ministry included a letter of instructions to the captives in Babylonia. Counseling them to be good citizens, he told them God would bring them home in his good time. Known as the "weeping prophet," because of his concern for the people of the covenant, he is also noted for his "confessions."

In some respects, Jeremiah was much like the majority of the prophets. Pointing out Judah's failure in keeping the covenant, he saw dire consequences ahead. In another respect, he reminds one of Habakkuk. Like Habakkuk, he questioned God. Mistreated at the hands of his enemies, he questioned why God had allowed it to happen (15:10–21), or why God had allowed him to be born (20:7–13).

In conclusion, Jeremiah taught that restoration for Judah would follow the judgment (30:4–22). Significantly, there would be a new covenant, one written on the heart rather than on stone (31:23–40). Once again, the themes of the Exodus and Covenant take an interesting turn here.

"Now arise, go forth from this land . . ."
Genesis 13:3

Chapter Nineteen
MOVING ON

Sometimes life is left in shambles. In seminary, the biblical archeology class was taught in a rather large but aging classroom. The room, which seated about two hundred, had a low, plaster ceiling. During the break for mid-morning chapel, the old ceiling gave way, dropping pounds of heavy plaster to the floor. Since class was not in session, no one was injured.

The world is not always so kind. The ceiling falls and often leaves life in shambles. Most of us initially do what the writer of Lamentations did: we mourn. But is there life after mourning?

I think you will appreciate what Mr. Floyd Dean did. You remember him, the beloved deacon from chapter 1. Floyd was running late for work. Entering his garage, he climbed into his four-door Chevrolet. Starting the car, he realized a back door was ajar. While reaching over to close the door, his foot accidentally hit the gas petal. Unfortunately, the shift was set in drive. The car shot forward, plowing through the back of the garage, but escaping without a scratch from the falling lumber stacked on each side. Lurching ahead on its journey, the Chevrolet dropped three feet to ground level and plowed its way toward the fence enclosing the back yard. Floyd braked the car as Ora, his pretty wife, quickly came to see about him. Anxiously she inquired, "Are you all right, honey? Are you all right?" Floyd, who was unhurt but thoroughly put out by the sequence of events, had had enough. He called out, "Just open the gate, Ora. Just open the gate." As the gate swung open, without uttering another word, Floyd roared the Chevrolet through the opening and shot down the street, not once looking back at the shambles left behind. What classic action!

The ceiling has a way of unexpectedly falling in upon us. At some point, preferably sooner rather than later, we must determine to move on. Paul put its this way, "Forgetting what lies behind, and straining forward to what lies ahead, I press on . . ." (Phil. 3:13–14).

Now may be an exceptionally good time to consider moving beyond a disaster in life.

LAMENTATIONS

Lamentations mourns the 587–86 B.C. destruction of Jerusalem by the Babylonians. The book is made up of five funeral poems expressing the grief of the writer. Describing the devastation, the author reminds Judah of the cause of Jerusalem's fall and cries out to the Lord for rescue and restoration from the wreckage.

Our overview at this point includes the beginning of the covenant people. At Mt. Sinai, they receive the Law. This occurs at the conclusion of their exodus from Egypt (Exodus). The covenant people look back with their universal questions. They recall their ancestors, the patriarchs (Genesis). Moving into Canaan, they conquer and settle the promised land (Joshua). Losing sight of their covenant relation with God, they enter a period of Dark Ages (Judges). Emerging from the Dark Ages, they reach new heights in the monarchy, but decline again in the divided kingdom (1 and 2 Samuel, 1 and 2 Kings, and 1 and 2 Chronicles). The prophets proclaim the desire of God to uphold the covenant people. They also chronicle their spiritual and ethical decline which ends first with the fall of the northern kingdom (722–721 B.C.), and then with the fall of the southern kingdom in 587–86 B.C. (Amos, Hosea, Isaiah, Micah, Zephaniah, Nahum, Habakkuk, and Jeremiah). Finally, there is the lament over the destruction of Jerusalem in Lamentations.

> "The word of the Lord came to me: 'What do you mean by repeating this proverb concerning the land of Israel, "The fathers have eaten sour grapes and the children's teeth are set on edge"? As I live, says the Lord God, this proverb shall no more be used by you in Israel.'"
> Ezekiel 18:1–3

Chapter Twenty
SPITTING OUT SOUR GRAPES

For a great part of their history, the people of the covenant thought in terms of the total community. The good of the community demanded their first loyalty. One of the examples of their fierce loyalty to the good of the community is found in the book of Joshua. There a man called Aachan violated the ban on plundering goods in the holy war against Jericho. His transgression caused him to lose his life, the lives of his loved ones, and the lives of his servants and animals. The community stoned Aachan and his family, believing his action caused them to lose the next battle in the war. His mistake had affected them all. His penalty was to lose everything he had, including his life. "Corporate responsibility" was meant to be first and foremost in everyone's mind.

In Ezekiel 18, a new emphasis emerged. It stands at the other end of the spectrum. It is "individual responsibility." It means each individual is important in the community. Particularly, it means that an individual is not to blame someone else for his or her plight, but is to accept personal responsibility. One's predecessors are not to be blamed by repeating the proverb, "The fathers have eaten sour grapes, and the children's teeth have been set on edge." The fathers are not to be held responsible, as though children of later generations could blame their iniquities on their parents, grandparents, or great grandparents. Rather, "The soul (individual) that sins shall die" (18:1–4). The responsibility is his or hers.

In our world, as we look for answers to the terrible tragedies across the country, Ezekiel would remind us that there is enough blame to go around. The key is individual responsibility and undertaking the arduous, generations-long task of teaching it to each soul. May we find grace to spit out sour grapes.

EZEKIEL

Ezekiel is an eccentric spokesman for Yahweh. Ezekiel often acted out his message rather than speaking it. He played war in miniature, symbolizing the siege and fall of Jerusalem. He was asked to lie on his side for extended time to symbolize the length of Israel's punishment. He cooked his food over dried manure to illustrate extreme conditions during the fall of Jerusalem, and he had his hair cut like a captive of war to symbolize the captivity. His extraordinary description of God in chapter 1 of his book is illustrative of his unusual vision.

The prophet saw the people of the covenant through the difficult period of Babylonian captivity. He assisted them in understanding how God could allow Jerusalem's fall. Ezekiel's message led them to a more mature faith and prepared them for their eventual return home. A well-known passage, found in Ezekiel 37, speaks of the restoration of the people. It describes dry, bleached bones of the dead, which God would put together once more, causing them to live again. Ezekiel proclaimed that Israel would survive the captivity and begin life as a people again!

"A friend loves at all times, and a brother is
born for adversity."
Proverbs 17:17

Chapter Twenty-One

A Reassuring Presence

Four-year-old Robby was proudly wearing the uniform he had just gotten in his second Ju Jitsu class. His father picked him up in his truck. Stopping at a truck stop, his dad went inside for a few moments. He left Robby in the nearby truck, where he could easily keep an eye on him. His son gave him something to see. Robby calmly climbed out of the truck and walked over to a burly, 250-pound trucker, a perfect stranger. With a challenging "ha yah," the Ju Jitsu novice served notice on the stranger. Just coming from class, Robby was ready to take the trucker on. Immediately taking his stance, Robby began making his moves. One after another, he placed several menacing chops in the air, all accompanied by appropriately aggressive noises. It was a show of strength, and the rough-looking stranger was duly impressed. In fact, he laughed uproariously, but not without great approval.

I am not sure how Robby would have reacted had the big stranger scowled at him or made retaliatory moves. But it is my judgment that Robby was considerably reinforced by the thought that his dad was just inside the store. In fact, he was probably undergirded by that reassurance from the very beginning of his adventure.

Isaiah reminded Israel that the great Creator was close by. Although in their case they may have forgotten it, the truth was that the One who was in charge of the very universe itself was at hand to bring hope.

When held captive by circumstances, needed assurance can often be given by someone who is simply willing to stand close by. Perhaps you have benefited from just such a presence yourself.

Today may be your chance to undergird someone else who could use the reassuring presence of a friend. Your willing presence may be all that is required.

2 ISAIAH

A second spokesman for Yahweh helped prepare the people for life after their captivity. He is sometimes referred to as 2 Isaiah, or as the unknown prophet. The book of Isaiah is sometimes thought of as having two parts. The latter part, chapters 40–66, is sometimes referred to as 2 Isaiah.

This prophet, like Ezekiel, was a prophet of encouragement. Interestingly enough, he gave his encouragement in the language of a second Exodus. Reclaiming the heritage of his people, he proclaimed that God is preparing a second time to lead them in an exodus from captivity. Picking up this major theme of the Old Testament, he reminds them that they are a people who have been delivered from slavery. Their deliverance will be continued now with a second Exodus. Being led back to their homeland, they will be able to rebuild their covenant relationship with God.

2 Isaiah related that the God who will initiate this Exodus is the very Creator of the universe. They are comforted and strengthened by this understanding. Even though they have been suppressed, they have a magnificent God who has not forgotten them.

In his further development of the theme, the prophet includes another picture. The covenant is now depicted in the language of servanthood. The four servant poems in his book represent a call to understand the covenant in terms of service both to God and man. The people are to be a "light to the nations" (49:4–6). Israel's role is now seen to be that of a servant, according to one of the poems.

In tying the Old Testament together at this point, it is apparent that we have come almost full circle in the story. Here in the sixth century B.C, the people are captives once again, ready to be taken on an Exodus back to the land of promise. It remains to be seen if they will repeat their history in the five hundred years or so before the appearance of the One some see as their deliverer.

> "Thou dost keep him in perfect peace whose mind is
> stayed on thee, because he trusts in thee."
> Isaiah 26:3

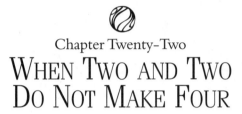

Chapter Twenty-Two

WHEN TWO AND TWO DO NOT MAKE FOUR

Some time ago I read that a man sued a church. He understood from the church's message that if he would tithe, he would receive material wealth in return. He tithed, and when he did not become wealthy, he sued the church for his money back. I never saw a follow-up article. I do not know how his case turned out.

There may have been those in Haggai's day who felt religion operated mechanically. This line of thinking says that if a person is good and does good things, good things will happen to him. If he is bad and does bad things, bad things will happen to him.

If some in the Old Testament entertained that notion early on, they were due to reexamine it later. Job is a good example. We'll consider the question again when we come to the book which bears his name. In this respect, the best commentary on the Old Testament is the Old Testament itself. It examines and then later reexamines issues of the people of the covenant, often in a new light.

But if rebuilding the Temple doesn't bring good fortune, where does that leave the matter of faith and worship? Specifically, what does it mean if good does not follow on the heels of doing good—when two and two do not make four? It probably means that life can be thoroughly devastating, as you probably well know, even in face of doing good.

But at the same time, the life of faith is all the more challenging. Life can also be filled with overwhelming surprise and great meaning. The challenge is to conceive of a God who can be trusted. The challenge is to conceive of and trust in a God who will ultimately triumph. No superficial transaction will make it so, however. No mechanical transaction will make it so. But deep, persevering trust will suggest, if not witness, the ultimate good. Apparently, the Old Testament is leading the reader in that direction.

HAGGAI

Assuming Abraham's story takes place about 2300 B.C., and the captives in Babylon were released to go home in 538 B.C., we have been constructing an Old Testament house for over seventeen hundred years. What does it look like?

The foundation of the house is the Exodus. The first building block laid on the foundation is the covenant made with Yahweh at Mt. Sinai. The next block is the people's recollection of their past, recorded in two parts—the universal questions about life and the recalling of their ancestors. Block number three is the conquest of the land of Canaan by the covenant people. Number four is the nearly two hundred years in which the people forgot their covenant. Number five is their flourishing monarchy, especially under King David. This is followed by block six—their decline, during which the nation split into two parts. Building block number seven is the fall of the northern part of the land to the Assyrians. And number eight is the fall of the southern part to the Babylonians. Nine is the captivity in Babylon. Number ten is the return home under the Persian King Cyrus. Finally, number eleven is the home-again experience, beginning with the book of Haggai. If your picture of the Old Testament house or structure has been hazy, perhaps the image is beginning to clear up at this point.

Haggai is concerned with one thing. He wants the home-again people to rebuild the Temple. This desire is interesting for several reasons. One is that during their approximately fifty years in captivity, they had no Temple. This absence was apparently replaced by another institution of worship, the synagogue. Worship in the synagogue was not built around sacrifice, but consisted of such elements as a call to worship, singing, and prayers.

The desire is interesting for a second reason. It concerns the prophets. Long before the captivity, the prophets had strongly resisted the abuse of sacrificial worship in the Temple. It had become a meaningless way to approach God. Simply stated, people offered an animal to be sacrificed without offering themselves. This prompted one prophet after another to speak out strongly against the system. In summary, they agreed that God did not want sacrifice. He wanted obedience.

In light of this background, it is interesting to see Haggai obsessed with the rebuilding of the Temple. The people have the synagogue. The people are poor and the land is poor. The residents of the land resent the returning captives, but Haggai calls for the rebuilding nonetheless.

The Temple is dedicated in 515 B.C. It in no way resembled Solomon's Temple. It did not begin to approximate the size or magnificence of the old Temple. It was a poor man's spot for sacrificial worship.

> "Render true judgments, show kindness and mercy each to
> his brother, do not oppress the widow, the fatherless, the
> sojourner, or the poor; and let none of you devise
> evil against his brother in your heart."
> Zechariah 7:9–10

Chapter Twenty-Three

A Snapshot of a Golden Age

Before the covenant people came home from exile, they had a beautiful picture of a homecoming painted for them by 2 Isaiah. And rightly so. However, the actual homecoming was attended by unexpected difficulties. Poverty, a poor welcome by the residents of the community (who resented their return), and the hardships of trying to start life over again were among some of the problems. Zechariah's message suggested a messianic age that would provide hope.

However, it is interesting that in Zechariah's total message, he includes a beautiful nugget of wisdom. If followed, it would provide a community with peace and prosperity. He wrote, "Render true judgments, show kindness and mercy each to his brother, do not oppress the widow, the fatherless, the sojourner, or the poor; and let none of you devise evil against his brother in your heart" (Zech. 7:9–10).

In light of this counsel, I watched as a bus pulled into a parking lot. The handicapped door opened and an attendant rolled a wheelchair-bound young man out of the bus and into the cafeteria. He was joined by a blind companion, and three or four other handicapped young people. With the group, there was a young blonde lady, whom you might have expected to see at the swimming pool or on the tennis court. Along with another helper, she was in charge of the group. As the group ate their lunches, I watched the young lady carefully feed the boy in the wheelchair, who nevertheless got food all over his face. She took a napkin and patiently cleaned his face over and over again. She and her companion attended to the particular needs of each person, neglecting no one. The group was cared for beautifully.

As they left, I thought of what a golden age must be like. I concluded that what I saw may not have been a scene from such a time. I had no doubt, however, that it was a picture of the beautiful spirit of Zechariah's passage. If followed, Zechariah's message would produce a golden age of its own, even today.

ZECHARIAH

Zechariah, another home-again prophet, joined Haggai. He also encouraged the people to rebuild the Temple. However, he did not emphasize the direct returns from building the Temple quite like his contemporary. His encouragement came in visions that he experienced. He envisioned the possibility of God breaking into the scene with the messianic age, or a golden age for the people. He saw the possibility of the time of a messianic king and a time of peace and prosperity. With that prospect, he strengthened the people in their task of rebuilding the community.

> "Commit your work to the Lord and your plans
> will be established."
> Proverbs 16:3

Chapter Twenty-Four

COMMERCE AND CARING

I was doing a book signing at Pugh's Pharmacy and Gifts. An attractive, middle-aged woman, wearing portable oxygen gear, examined one of the books. "I could not have made it, had it not been for them." She was referring to the owners, Wilton DePriest, who was also the pharmacist, and Gayle, his pretty wife. It was obvious she was referring to more than the prescriptions and medical supplies. As the day progressed, I heard the same statement from scores of individuals. I heard it from troubled teens, victims of alcohol and drug abuse, war veterans, the elderly, the poor and displaced, and countless others. At the tables in the refreshment area, they came deliberately for counsel. They came for support. They came for affirmation and reaffirmation. They came daily for various kinds of help.

Without question, Pugh's was literally bustling with business. It is a place of constant commerce. But obviously there is something else that is important to the proprietors. It is a subtle place of real ministry. Wilton and Gayle provide a genuine combination of commerce and caring. Their customers will readily tell you.

As Ezra led the home-again people to rebuild, he was faced with combining the same two elements: caring and commerce. The people of the covenant needed both.

Today's individuals need no less. The chance may arise to provide genuine caring in the midst of our own commerce. And whether we do so or not may be far more important than we realize. We may enable persons "to make it."

EZRA

Although a messianic king did not emerge in the home-again community, a priest did. In fact, the priest became the key religious and political figure in the community. Ezra, the priest, filled that role so well he earned for himself the title "the father of Judaism." Moreover, since Judah had been the portion of the kingdom that was in captivity, the returnees were referred to as Jews from that time onward.

Under the priest, the covenant was reaffirmed, and the law of the covenant was prominent. Once again there was a retelling of the story of the Exodus and the deliverance of the people from slavery. The parallel to the original story and their recent experiences must have been especially significant for this home-again community.

"Let us rise up and build."
Nehemiah 2:18

Chapter Twenty-Five

Jump-Starting Life

Many years ago I visited an individual in an institution well-known for its treatment of mental problems. A common treatment was shock therapy. It seemed to assist the individual by separating him from an awareness of elements in his past. It often seemed to provide a jump-start for new life.

Sometimes life can be jump-started. It may be done even when life seems like a hopeless mess of ups and downs, rights and wrongs, hurts and hopes, successes and failures. Of course, it cannot be completely untangled with one giant motion. But, with a determined effort at covenant in a marriage or social relationship, two can make a single step to walk together. The hopelessness is then reduced by one step. And sometimes a single step is enough to begin building life again. Step by step, the mess can be undone.

Is life a mess? Perhaps you can think of one step to jump-start it in the right direction. Then take that single step today.

NEHEMIAH

In Nehemiah, we find a fourth home-again figure. He is also concerned with making a new beginning in the land of Palestine. Before considering Nehemiah, however, think about the overview of the Old Testament at this point. The building blocks can be stacked in larger units. First, the foundation of the Old Testament is the first five books (the Pentateuch). The story here includes the Exodus, the receiving of the law at Sinai, the look back at the ancestors, and a look at beginnings.

The second large unit is the conquest and settling of Canaan and the Dark Ages in Joshua and Judges. This may be thought of as the framing of the Old Testament house.

The third large unit consists of the people as a monarchy, and the monarchy divided into two parts. This unit may be thought of as the roof, at first providing shelter for the covenant people (1 and 2 Samuel, 1 and 2 Kings, and 1 and 2 Chronicles).

The fourth unit is a premature crumbling of the Old Testament building with an approximate fifty-year period of captivity (the Prophets). But even in the captivity, building blocks were being formed to be used on returning home—the synagogue, learning to speak the Aramaic language, and becoming merchants. Apparently the people had also emphasized the writing of their oral history during the exile.

And now a fifth unit, with the previous four in place, works to give further shape to the Old Testament house (Haggai, Zechariah, Ezra, and now Nehemiah).

Persia, having taken over Babylonia, was now in control of Palestine. Nehemiah, who served as cup-bearer to the king of Persia, was appointed governor of the home-again people. With the support of the king, he went home to rebuild the walls of Jerusalem. He set out to rebuild the structure of the covenant life, as well as the physical structures.

One of the problems he addressed was the marriage of covenant people with outsiders. The particular manner he used to address them was to dismantle the marriages and send the outsiders back to their homes. It must have been a particularly difficult procedure. He also addressed problems related to tithes and the Sabbath.

> "I will give to the Lord the thanks due to his righteousness,
> and I will sing praise to the name of the Lord, the Most High."
> Psalm 7:17

Chapter Twenty-Six

A Gratitude Party

Several couples were invited to the home of Gene and Sue Greer, our neighbors. The purpose of the invitation was not told. Earlier in the week, a prankster suggested that Sue was expecting a baby, although everyone knew that was not the case. Much good-natured ribbing followed during the week. Not knowing the reason for the invitation, several in the group brought cards and items for a baby shower. Great fun developed as each gift and card was opened.

But after refreshments, Sue told the real reason for the gathering. She had asked the group to her home to thank them. It was a gratitude party. Sue had experienced difficult physical challenges. She continued to experience them daily, although from her great positive attitude and cheerful demeanor, it could never be guessed. At the same time, her neighbors had provided definite comfort and encouragement. She wanted to thank them, so she gave a gratitude party. How appropriately significant!

If we surround ourselves with people like Malachi's contemporaries, a happy future may elude us, and we can complain and become cynical just like them. But there is another choice. We can give a gratitude party. We can choose to enumerate the reasons we have for being thankful. Obviously, the choice is ours. We can complain, or we can be thankful. But there is a world of difference in the life each choice produces.

MALACHI

About the time of Ezra and Nehemiah (500–450 B.C.), Malachi addressed the disillusionment of the home-again people. Their happy return had been marred by numerous problems. This spokesman spoke to a complaining people who were tired of waiting for their great future to unfold. Malachi's message is given in the form of a question and answer session between the people and God. With a high regard for the covenant, he addressed their complaints about God's supposed injustice, their disrespect in worship, their faithlessness in marriage, and their neglect of tithes and offerings. Malachi closed by speaking of a "messenger" (3:1), who would prepare the people for the coming of the Lord to his Temple.

"Answer not a fool according to his folly, lest you be like him yourself. Answer a fool according to his folly lest he be wise in his own eyes."
Proverbs 26:4–5

Chapter Twenty-Seven

The Opportunity of a Dilemma

An interesting passage is found in Proverbs 26:4–5. The verses give conflicting answers to the question, "How does one deal with a fool?" On one hand, the reader is counseled, "Answer not a fool according to his folly, lest you be like him yourself." On the other hand, he is instructed to "Answer a fool according to his folly, lest he be wise in his own eyes."

The passages leave the reader uncertain about how to relate to a fool. But this is true only if the reader thinks of managing life by applying unyielding rules. The dilemma of the conflicting answers disappears when the reader uses his or her own judgement as to whether in a particular setting, he or she is to "answer a fool" or whether he or she is to "answer not a fool."

These passages seem to open up the possibility of thinking of Old Testament faith, at least at this point, in terms other than rigid, legalistic rules. Here the reader is asked to become a responsible participant in the decision-making process. When that happens, one's faith becomes more difficult, but far more satisfying at the same time.

Probably some of us have a problem at the moment, to which we would like to apply a ready-made solution. There is no such solution available, or there are conflicting answers. But by resorting to prayerful deliberations, we may produce an inward strength that no mechanical answer could ever produce. Perhaps we should accept the dilemma as an opportunity.

PROVERBS

Another building unit begins with Proverbs. It is the first of three wisdom books that make up the unit. The book itself is a collection of wisdom sayings, many of them brief and pointed. It is expected that the people of the covenant will follow the proverbs and, therefore, be wise. They will be blessed if they do. Of course, those who do not follow the proverbs are considered fools, and they cannot expect to be blessed.

The sayings fall into the category of practical wisdom. They are looked upon as basic common sense, or "horse sense." They apply to religious, civic, family, and personal life. Therefore, they cover a wide range of topics. The diverse range of topics discussed includes discipline, the needs of youth, wicked women, relationships, and motherhood.

In the last analysis, Proverbs gives the member of the covenant community concise advice on how to successfully get along in the everyday world.

> "In my distress I called upon the Lord; to my God I cried for help. From his temple he heard my voice, and my cry to him reached his ears."
> Psalm 18:6

Chapter Twenty-Eight

SUFFERING'S EXTENDED SHELF LIFE

Luther and Louise Drummond owned a music store in Nashville, Tennessee. They were faithful church and choir members. They sang duets in their own church and elsewhere by request. They led busy lives with heavy participation in business and social interests, as well as church life. With the passing years, they sold their business and retired. Later, they were forced to sell their home, which they could no longer keep up. They moved to a retirement high rise. There, the years have slowly taken their natural toll. The other day, Louise wrote a little note to say, "Luther's eyesight continues to fade. I've developed some heart problems, so we are hanging on—one day at a time."

Unfortunately, some suffering has a long shelf life. It is not completed with devastating swiftness. Its pain, uncertainty, and scariness plod slowly through mind and body day after day. There is no patent medicine to effect a quick cure. There is no patent answer, either. But there is God. This is the same God about whom Job concluded, "I know that thou canst do all things, and that no purpose of thine can be thwarted" (42:2). This is the same God to whom Job ultimately responded by saying, "I had heard of thee by the hearing of the ear, but now my eye sees thee" (42:5). He had heard of God with his ears, but his experience of suffering led him to uniquely trust in God.

Luther and Louise are addressing the pain of extended shelf lives by hanging on one day at a time. Like Job, they have a suffering trust. This can be our help as well. It is not a perfect answer, but it is a significant one.

JOB

Job examines anew the thought that righteous men prosper and bad men suffer. Job is introduced to the reader as a good and righteous man. Yet he suffers terribly through the loss of his seven sons and three daughters, his livestock, his wealth, and finally his own physical well-being. He is righteous and faithful, but he suffers.

Three friends, Eliphaz, Bildad, and Zophar, visit Job and declare the old understanding. They tell Job that he must be unrighteous, or he would not be suffering as he is. If he would repent of his sins, they counseled, he would be made well. But Job maintained consistently that he was a righteous and good man.

In rejecting the old idea, the reader is left with the understanding that a person can indeed be good and yet not prosper, but suffer. We are left with the realization that bad things can happen to good people.

In the book of Job, the resolution of the problem is basically twofold. First, Job is a man and not God. God's ways are not man's ways. Man cannot fully understand God, and therefore man cannot comprehend the problem of suffering. Secondly, God is all-wise and just. In man's experience, however, he can encounter God personally and perhaps move from a focus on suffering to a focus on faith.

There is a traditional ending to the story. Job's health and wealth are restored, along with seven new sons and three new daughters, and twice as many animals. The real answer to Job's problem is not here, but in the preceding paragraph.

> "My son, if you receive my words and treasure up my
> commandments with you . . . then you will understand the
> fear of the Lord and find the knowledge of God."
> Proverbs 2:1, 5

Chapter Twenty-Nine
A Meaningful Life

Given their different perspectives, it is interesting that Job and Ecclesiastes are joined as wisdom books. One is overtaken by sheer suffering; the other by sheer meaninglessness. We probably would not want to trade places with either. Suffering appears in many forms. Addressing a patient, one physician is said to have inquired, "Do you believe in God?" "Why do you ask?" responded his patient. "I am convinced," the physician continued, "that if you do not find God—something in whom or in which you can passionately believe—I am convinced that you will die."

Some of Ecclesiastes' predecessors in the Old Testament found a passionate faith in Yahweh, and that faith gave their lives meaning. They did not debate the issue of God's existence, or his involvement in their lives. They simply began with the first words in the book of Genesis, "In the beginning God. . . ." God was the beginning and the conclusion of all matters. In between was meaningful life.

May we be as fortunate as some of Ecclesiastes' predecessors in a discovery of meaningful life.

ECCLESIASTES

Ecclesiastes is the third of the wisdom voices among the home-again people, following Proverbs and Job.

This writer represents a departure from the usual thinking in the Old Testament. Earlier, Habakkuk had also departed from it. You will recall that he questioned God, asking why God had acted as he had. In the wisdom writings, Job challenged the orthodox thinking about suffering, and Ecclesiastes offers a pessimistic outlook on life. "Vanities of vanities . . .! All is vanity," the writer states at the beginning (1:2). He had tried work, wisdom, and then pleasure, but they were all worthless and did not satisfy him.

He has been called a deist, or one who believed in God, but thought that God has very little—if anything at all—to do with the world.

His understanding of history was also a departure from the usual. Instead of history moving to the good conclusion that God intended, this writer thought of history as moving in a circle, going nowhere (3:1–15). Good as well as bad persons received the same fate in life (9:2–12).

Orthodox responses to his unusual ideas do emerge from time to time. An example is found in 2:24–26. "There is nothing better for a man than that he should eat and drink, and find enjoyment in his toil. . . . For to the man who pleases him God gives wisdom and knowledge and joy. . . ."

Ecclesiastes, as well as Job, reminds us that not all home-again Jews thought alike about God.

"Let your fountain be blessed, and rejoice in the wife of your youth, a lovely hind, a graceful doe. Let her affection fill you at all times with delight, be infatuated always with her love."
Proverbs 5:18–19

Chapter Thirty
LOVE SONGS

Realizing their nakedness, Adam and Eve covered themselves in Genesis. From this account, interpreters have sometimes found sexual sin at the heart of the account, rather than disobedience. Such interpretation has colored the interpretation of the Old Testament elsewhere.

In America, the widespread attention given to sex on television, in advertising, and elsewhere has soaked the fabric of life. This, along with an abuse of sex, makes a consideration of the matter in Song of Songs difficult. The life and times of Solomon, whose name is sometimes used to title the book (Song of Solomon), may seem an easier background for discussing the book. After all, he is said to have had seven hundred wives and three hundred concubines.

Appreciating the value of these love songs may not be easy. We may simply wish they were not there. However, reading them in the loving relationship of the husband and his bride can give beautiful meaning for our culture.

> How fair and pleasant you are,
> O loved one, delectable maiden!
> You are stately as a palm tree,
> and your breasts are like its clusters,
> I say I will climb the palm tree

and lay hold of its branches.
Oh, may your breasts be like clusters of the vine,
and the scent of your breath like apples,
and your kisses like the best wine
that goes down smoothly,
gliding over lips and teeth (7:6–9 RSV).

SONG OF SONGS

Looking at the post-exile picture of the Old Testament, two building blocks have emerged. The first is made up of books devoted to rebuilding the community. The five rebuilding books are Ezra, Nehemiah, Malachi, Haggai, and Zechariah. The second building block is made up of the three wisdom books. They are Proverbs, Job, and Ecclesiastes.

The next "home-again" book, Song of Songs, is unusual. No earlier book is similar. God is not mentioned, and physical love is the theme of the writing. This theme has made the interpretation difficult for both Jews and Christians. Sometimes an allegorical interpretation has been favored. The bride is understood to be the church, and Jesus is the husband.

However, if we understand physical love positively, the book is actually a series of love songs. The writing recognizes that sex is a part of God's creation and is to be appreciated and honored accordingly.

> "Let not loyalty and faithfulness forsake you; bind them about your neck, write them on the tablet of your heart."
> Proverbs 3:3

Chapter Thirty-One

Exercises in Remembering

It is not surprising that several of the Psalms celebrate the themes of the covenant and the Exodus. Such songs are an exercise in remembering. They are songs of refreshment in faith.

> O God, when thou didst go forth before thy people,
> When thou didst march through the wilderness,
> The earth quaked, the heavens poured down rain,
> at the presence of God;
> Yon Sinai quaked at the presence of God, the God
> of Israel (Ps. 68:7–8).

> Our fathers, when they were in Egypt, did not consider
> thy wonderful works;
> They did not remember the abundance of thy steadfast love,
> But rebelled against the Most High at the Red Sea.
> Yet he saved them for his name's sake,
> That he might make known his mighty power (Ps. 106:7–8).

Perhaps we do not think of songbooks or hymnbooks as refresher courses in our faith. Try it, if you will. Pick a favorite hymn and listen to a rehearsal of your faith. It can be the needed refreshment for the start of the day. I'll join you.

Faith of our fathers! living still
In spite of dungeon, fire, and sword,
O how our hearts beat high with joy
When-e'er we hear that glorious word!
Faith of our fathers, holy faith!
We will be true to thee till death.
—Frederick W. Faber

PSALMS

The Psalms are the songs of the covenant people. They cover a time from early in their history, perhaps reaching even into the home-again period.

Like the Pentateuch, they are divided into five parts. Introduced by the first Psalm, they are concluded with a benediction in Psalm 150. In between, the five parts are marked by benedictions in chapters 41, 72, 89, 106, and 150.

The Psalms are associated with worship. They express thanksgiving, praise, pleas for help in a variety of problems, and honor to the king. They express to God the deep feelings of the covenant people. The Psalms create a picture of people coming to grips with life's struggle, set forth in poetic form. David and other figures are designated as the speaking principals.

> "Be not wise in your own eyes; fear the Lord, and turn away from evil. It will be healing to your flesh and refreshment to your bones."
> Proverbs 3:7–8

Chapter Thirty-Two

TOWARD HEALING

The speaker explained that pushing pins into the voodoo doll did not affect the person in whose image it was made. Rather the pins pierced the very hate that drove the person to push them in. Each pin was an exercise in healing, for it was driven into one's own hate in an effort to overcome it, she suggested.

Examining Obadiah, it is apparent that the prophet is giving vent to his hatred. Hopefully, his expression of it was the first step toward overcoming it. Whether or not that was the case with Obadiah, it can be the case with ill will. Venting it through writing allows one to follow up by throwing it away, literally and symbolically. It seems that before hatred can be eliminated, it must be expressed, at least to one's self. Such controlled venting may open the door to the healing of our own hatred. Rather than hurting someone else, we have an opportunity to forgive what we can acknowledge and express, hard though that may be.

OBADIAH

Obadiah has been called a "hymn of hate," the Edomites being the object of hatred. On their way to Canaan, Edom had apparently opposed the covenant people's attempt to use the King's Highway through their country. The ill will between the two peoples is clearly documented in Amos and elsewhere in the Old Testament.

The Book of Obadiah may have been written after the fall of Jerusalem to Babylon, for Edom had apparently celebrated after the city fell. Now Obadiah anticipates the fall of Edom. The prime purpose of the book is to celebrate the downfall of the Edomites. The Day of the Lord would include the toppling of Edom. The Jews could then happily celebrate.

"He who walks in integrity walks securely..."
Proverbs 10:9

Chapter Thirty-Three
Building Resolve

Joel's plague of locusts signaled the future coming of the Day of the Lord. The devastation of a recent hurricane here in the U.S. was no such signal. However, as I watched a coastal resident look at the scattered remains of her destroyed house, with Joel she raised her eyes beyond the present disaster to a future hope. Looking at the scene with great calm, she said simply, "We'll just have to build it back." If there were any sense of defeat or despair, it never showed.

How does disaster produce such resolve? Is it that the resolve, by faith and commitment, has been cultivated through the years? Disaster is the signal that reminds us to tap into the resolve. The pool is already there.

We cannot anticipate many of life's catastrophes. But we can quietly build small pieces of resolve daily, through a faith commitment in God. Maybe the best we can do is resolve to give our very best effort to the challenge life presents today.

JOEL

The spokesmen, or prophets, told of how God directed his people toward his good end, through the work of men and events. The apocalyptic writers succeeded the prophets. They told the story in a different way. Evil, which was intensely powerful, was confronted and overcome when God personally addressed it. In telling the story in this fashion, they used a particular set of tools. The tools consisted of numbers used as symbols, oftentimes in a code only the intended readers understood. There were pictures of strange creatures, having a combination of human and beastly or birdlike qualities. Striking imagery was used, and poetic description was paramount. With the apocalyptic writers, everything was written first, and thus meant to be read. With the prophets, everything was spoken first, to be heard, and then later it was written.

One great theme was at the heart of apocalyptic writing. It was written to encourage the faithful followers of the covenant in time of trouble. The tools used to say it were window dressing for the dominant message. The purpose of the writings was never meant to confuse or discourage the reader.

The book of Joel, like the prophets, spoke of the Day of the Lord. It was to be ushered in through a plague of locusts. But the picture was joined by apocalyptic language telling of an earthquake, an inability to see the sun and moon, and the disappearance of the stars (Joel 2:10–11). In the end, though, God brings prosperity to his people.

Joel represents a bridge from the prophets to the apocalyptic writers in the Old Testament. His book contains elements of both kinds of writing.

> "I cry aloud to the Lord, and he answers me
> from his holy hill."
> Psalm 3:4

Chapter Thirty-Four
HOPELESSNESS DISPELLED

The World War II POW told of a remarkable experience in prison camp. The camp was a place of lying, stealing, and betrayal. Each person strove for the slightest advantage. It was an environment of utter despair.

Two men began a worship service. They had no Bible, but each recalled Bible verses, putting together an oral Bible. They sang hymns from memory and spoke of their faith in terms of mutual helpfulness, trust, sharing, and caring. They pledged themselves again to living the life of faith. One by one, men began to join the service. They began to commit themselves to live responsibly also. Amazingly, the atmosphere of hopelessness was dispelled. Life, if not good, became bearable. It was characterized by hope.

Hope wears many faces. One of the faces shows an active trust in the God of a better tomorrow. Today may seem hopeless, but tomorrow can bring hope. Our active trust is the instrument of hope.

DANIEL

The Book of Daniel, along with Joel and chapters 9–14 of Zechariah, make up the apocalyptic building block of the Old Testament.

Like some other apocalyptic materials, Daniel includes visions, beasts from the sea, symbolic figures, numerology, and a last days theme. There are also stories of Daniel, Shadrach, Meshach, and Abednego.

The stories, set in the background of the Babylonian Exile, were probably put into their present form during the persecution of Antiochus Epiphanes (175–163 B.C.).

The book of Daniel was meant to bring hope and encouragement to the people of the covenant during a time of great trial and discouragement.

> "If your enemy is hungry, give him bread to eat, and
> if he is thirsty, give him water to drink . . ."
> Proverbs 25:21

Chapter Thirty-Five

INCLUDING OUTSIDERS

The humorist spoke lovingly of growing up in a large family in a crowded immigrant section of New York City. His parents and numerous brothers and sisters were crammed into a small apartment in a big apartment building during the Great Depression. They had little material goods. His mother, however, always managed to place food on the table to feed the family. If others showed up at mealtime, as they often did, she simply watered down the soup a little more. One uncle managed to appear consistently at mealtime. Each time he was politely asked to stay for dinner. And each time he politely replied, "Well, I have already eaten at home, but I guess I will just snack a little." He promptly seated himself and proceeded to eat more than anyone else at the table. The scene was repeated too many times for one nephew to count. Finally, on one such occasion, the nephew said to his uncle, "Uncle, have you ever thought about eating with us and just snacking a little at your own house?"

I'm not sure the nephew's suggestion caused the uncle to change his eating habits. But it never changed the willingness of the immigrant family to welcome outsiders into the family circle.

Is there someone who needs to be welcomed into the warmth and understanding of our circle?

ESTHER

The last Old Testament building block reflects two views toward those who are outside the ranks of the covenant people. The first excludes outsiders and is called particularism. The second, called universalism, favors the inclusion of outsiders.

Esther falls into the first category, urging the people to care for themselves exclusively. Esther, the Jewish bride of the Persian king, persuaded the king to allow all Jews to defend themselves against their enemies. In a nationalistic purge they wiped out their enemies all over the land. The feast that celebrated the event is called Purim. The book seems to have been written to explain the origin of this feast.

> "Entreat me not to leave you or to return from following you;
> for where you go, I will go, ..."
> Ruth 1:16

Chapter Thirty-Six
NITTY-GRITTY LOVE

Courtship and marriage customs change: consider the story of Ruth. Newly widowed, Ruth returns with her mother-in-law to Israel, and she follows the reapers to glean bits of grain to take home. On discovering who Ruth is, Boaz, who is Naomi's kinsman, suggests that Ruth follow his reapers more closely to gather more grain. And Naomi, on learning of Boaz's interest in Ruth, plays cupid. She instructs Ruth in the customary way of letting Boaz know of her interest in him. Naomi tells Ruth to get cleaned up, put on her perfume and best clothes, and go to Boaz's threshing floor in the evening. At the time for retirement, she is to lie down at Boaz's feet and then uncover his feet. She follows these instructions. When he responded with, "Who are you?" she answered, "I am Ruth, your maidservant; spread your skirt over your maidservant if you are next of kin." Her words meant, "Take me for your wife." He agreed, and they became engaged. The next day he stood in the city gate as a kinsman and took care of matters to lawfully make her his bride.

There is a reminder here. Love has its trimmings, such as the engagement, rings, cakes, weddings, or counterparts in other cultures and times. These trimmings are loved and sought after. But they are not love. We see both the trimmings and love in Ruth, but the significant feature of Ruth is its genuine portrayal of love's real nature—its nitty-gritty nature. Listen to it in the speech that

Ruth made to Naomi, often used in the marriage ceremony, but offered originally from a daughter-in-law to a mother-in-law: "Entreat me not to leave you or to return from following you; for where you go I will go, and where you lodge I will lodge; your people shall be my people, and your God my God; where you die I will die, and there will I be buried. May the Lord do so to me and more also if even death parts me from you" (Ruth 1:16).

Nitty-gritty love may be applied to many relationships. It works between mothers-in-law and daughters-in-law, husbands and wives, and even among siblings.

RUTH

If Esther favored particularism, or excluding outsiders during the late, home-again period, the book of Ruth favored including them. This position has been called universalism.

Although the date of the book may be much later, the setting for Ruth is the period of the Judges. It tells the story of Ruth, King David's great-grandmother, to indicate that the Jews should not be narrow in their view of other nations.

The story is of Naomi, a Jewess who had been taken by her husband Elimelech to live in Moab during a time of famine in Israel. He died, leaving Naomi in a foreign country with her two sons. The boys married Moabite women, Orpah and Ruth. Like their father, the sons died, leaving the three women. Naomi decided to return home. Her two daughters-in-law wished to go with her. Only Ruth actually returned home with her, however.

Once in Israel, Ruth married Boaz, a kinsman of Elimelech, and according to the story, they became the great-grandparents of King David. The point of the story, of course, is that David's ancestor, Ruth, was a foreigner, suggesting that the people could not claim to be a pure-blooded people or to be an exclusive people.

"Let another praise you, and not your own mouth;
a stranger, and not your own lips."
Proverbs 27:2

Chapter Thirty-Seven
Not a Vanity Plate

The license plate read URLVD. In today's world, one might have expected IMLVD, or a similar self-appreciation slogan. Instead, the driver had paid for a statement that expressed appreciation for anyone who read it. It was a generous and gracious act.

It is not easy to be inclusive of others in the formation of our thoughts. It is much easier to be exclusive. In fact, the challenge of faith is the realization that all men are the material from which God's kingdom is formed.

JONAH

Jonah also represents a non-exclusive or universalist attitude toward outsiders. Nineveh, capital and symbol of Assyria, had treated the people of the covenant with great cruelty when they defeated them and took them captive. Therefore it is not surprising that when Jonah was asked to go to the city of Nineveh with the message of repentance and acceptance, he tried to run away from the task. Unable to do so, he camped out in the shade of a large plant to await Nineveh's fall. However, his vigil was undone when a worm ate away the root of the plant, causing it to die. Jonah was left to suffer miserably from the elements. More importantly, God exposed Jonah to his error of failing to carry "light" to the non-Jewish world.

The book of Jonah joins the book of Ruth in the understanding that God's love is not an exclusive Jewish commodity, but is meant for all people.

Part 2

THE NEW TESTAMENT

> "And a young man followed him with nothing but a linen cloth about his body; and they seized him, but he left the linen cloth and ran away naked."
> Mark 14:51–52

Chapter Thirty-Eight

EMERGING FROM THE SHADOWS

There is an unusual and rather amusing picture found in two brief statements in Mark. It occurs as Jesus is being arrested, prior to his trial and subsequent death. It describes a young man standing in the shadows, apparently watching the arrest. The arresting authorities, believing that he was a follower of Jesus, attempted to arrest him also. As they reached to apprehend him, however, he quickly moved away. They did manage to grasp his loincloth, the only piece of clothing he was wearing. The resulting picture was of a loincloth dangling from the hands of the authorities and a young man dashing to safety in the buff. Had comedian Ray Stevens described the scene he may have captioned it, "The First Streaker Mentioned in the Gospels."

The brief story can be easily lifted from its context without affecting the account of the gospel. This fact has caused mild speculation that the author of the gospel is this young man. He was embarrassed by the event and would not give his name. He inserted the brief account to let the reader know he was there, however. This speculation has little basis for support, but it is an intriguing thought.

A more pertinent thought may concern the young man's standing in the shadows. It must have been a frightening scene. Most of us would have stood with him, I imagine. Even Jesus' disciples soon withered under its impact, with Peter denying his discipleship repeatedly.

Most of the calls to become involved in life are not nearly so dramatic or dangerous. Some of the calls are as commonplace as the challenge to get off the couch to actively participate in life. To find the courage to leave one's rooms to share in church or social activities. To discover the will to begin again after a great loss or a major setback. To rise above stinging words, a rebuff, or a put-down of some sort. To emerge from the shadows of mild paranoia and to stride into life.

It is not surprising that a common element in the refusal to move into life is the fear of failure. Words from two presidents of the last century are meaningful in conclusion. Franklin Roosevelt reminded his audience during WWII that "the only thing we have to fear is fear itself." Earlier, Theodore Roosevelt appropriately concluded that it is far better to engage life in the arena, experiencing its sweat and blood, than to stand on the sidelines, merely watching life unfold.

May great determination and strength be ours to engage life!

MARK

There are four gospels in the New Testament, although we have knowledge of other written documents. In some cases, we have little more than a reference to a writing. In others, the gospel or some part of it is available. The Gospel of Thomas is one example.

Of these written documents, Matthew, Mark, Luke, and John are included in the canon. That is, the church considered these four to be authoritative.

The author of the book of Mark is anonymous. The same thing can be said about Matthew, Luke, and John. The names that have been assigned these gospels have come from church tradition. The documents themselves have no authors mentioned. In the case of Mark's Gospel, tradition has assigned authorship to John Mark, who accompanied Paul in his missionary work. According to an early source, Mark was heavily dependent upon Simon Peter as a source of information for his Gospel.

Obviously, Mark is being considered first here, as it is in most discussions of the four books. It is thought to be the first one written, possibly around 65–70 A.D. Among the several reasons for this date is that Matthew and Luke seem to use portions of Mark in their Gospels. Also, Mark doesn't refer directly to the destruction of the Temple in 70 A.D. Mathew and Luke seem to allude to the event, suggesting that Mark's Gospel was written prior to the destruction and that Matthew and Luke wrote afterward. But when Mathew's Gospel appeared with its more complete account of the gospel, it became widely used, and eventually took Mark's place as the first-mentioned of the four.

Each of the four books presents Jesus from the author's particular perspective. In Mark, the emphasis is upon Jesus' deeds, miracles, and works. The Gospel includes relatively little of the teachings of Jesus. It is his mighty works that usher in God's kingdom, bringing relief for the suffering of mankind.

Moreover, Mark's perspective gives much attention to the humanity of Jesus. If the author had used the words of the writer of Hebrews, he would have said of Jesus, "He was tempted in every respect even as we are." This picture of Jesus' humanity allows the author to show Jesus as a victim who is crucified. His bond with humanity reached to death itself. And as a climax, there is victory over suffering and death, in his resurrection.

The gospel, or good news, is that one can follow Jesus in life. Commitment to him gives salvation. At the same time, however, following Jesus may mean following him in persecution and death as well. In fact, a prime purpose of Mark may have been to prepare Jesus' followers throughout the Roman Empire for persecution. This is especially probable if he were writing from Rome, where local persecution of the church took place under Nero. Mark wanted to warn the church that following Jesus could possibly include persecution and death. Perhaps this was Mark's perspective when he penned the Gospel bearing his name.

"Trust in the Lord with all your heart, and do not rely on your own insight. In all your ways acknowledge him and he will make straight your paths."
Proverbs 3:5–6

Chapter Thirty-Nine
SO MANY CHOICES

The old country store displayed candy that had been popular years before. Packaged in clear plastic bags was a bountiful assortment: curled licorice sticks; small yellow and red wrapped pieces of Dubble-Bubble gum; blue, yellow, white, red, and green gum balls; black-striped peanut butter crunches, coconut cheweys, and more. Remember the candy counter challenges of childhood? So much candy. So little money. What to buy?

That may have been how people felt when they were presented with the person and message of Jesus. In the matter of religion, they had been overloaded already. The Jewish world was filled with diverse viewpoints from the Pharisees, Sadducees, Essenes, and Herodians. There were also the ideas of Platonism, Stoicism, Epicureanism, the Mystery Religions, and much more. And then there was Jesus.

Not unlike the first century, we may be experiencing religion overload. The western world has seen the growth of many religions that previously were not very visible. So many religions. So many choices.

In light of this, it is helpful to know that Jesus was not about the business of adding to a person's stressful overload. The Pharisees had already done that. Others may have increased the confusion.

Obviously, choices can be confusing. Yet God is not a God of confusion. Belief or trust provides the very opposite of confusion. Commitment offers peace. May trust and peace be yours today.

MATTHEW

Matthew may have written his Gospel to add the teachings of Jesus to Mark's account of Jesus' deeds. This more complete account pictured Jesus as the Messiah or anointed deliverer. Directed to a Jewish audience, it attempted to convince the audience of Jesus' messiahship.

Tradition has attributed authorship to Matthew, also identified as Levi, the tax collector. The writer's tendency to carefully organize his work into orderly groups may indicate a profession such as tax-collecting, given to neat and meticulous categories. For example, the book seems to fall easily into five divisions, each division marked by the phrase, "And when Jesus finished these sayings . . ." (7:28, 11:1, 13:53, 19:1, and 26:1). However, some scholars doubt this authorship because it seems strange that Matthew, who was one of the twelve disciples, would have relied so heavily upon the account of Mark, who was not an apostle.

The divisions of the book may or may not point to the assumed orderliness of a tax collector author. At the same time, the division of the book into five basic parts may indicate something else. The book may tie into the theme of the Old Testament, relating Matthew and the Gospels to the Old Testament and a continuation of the story we have been following. Dividing his book into five parts may have been intended to say to his Jewish readers that the revered Pentateuch of their faith had now been followed by the "new Pentateuch." The old Law had been replaced by the new Law, with Jesus as the new Moses. The church was the new Israel. Moreover, the New Covenant, spoken of by Jeremiah, had now begun in Jesus. Meeting with his disciples before the crucifixion, he "took a cup, and when he had given thanks, he gave it to them saying, 'Drink of it, all of you, for this is my blood of the covenant . . .'" (Matt. 26:27).

Written after the destruction of Jerusalem and before 115 A.D. (when it is quoted by Ignatius of Antioch), the Gospel of Matthew provided the church with a manual of instruction for its life.

Matthew and the other gospel writers continue the story of the Old Testament. They present an update of the story to the descendants of the people who exited Egypt, along with those who joined them later. It becomes clear that the concepts of Exodus and Covenant provide our overview of the Bible right into the Gospels.

"Make a joyful noise to the Lord, all the land! Serve the Lord
with gladness! Come into his presence with singing."
Psalm 100:1

Chapter Forty
A Hymn-Singing Church

Through the years, the singing of hymns has provided a way for the church to proclaim its faith—to understand and share its message. It has incidentally provided some mischievous youngsters an avenue of mirth. For example, the song "Blessed Be the Tie that Binds" was known to lack a certain syncopation as it was sung in my church. On one such occasion, the majority of the congregation ended their singing a note or two before another smaller, but rather loud group of singers did. Teenagers sitting in the back of the congregation made up the loud group. This group accomplished their disruption by allowing the congregation to sing "Blessed be the tie that binds," while they sang only "Blessed be the tie." Then belatedly singing the words "that binds" after a pause, and singing all of the words of the song as did the congregation, allowed the teens to remain two notes behind everyone else. They were then able to sing the phrase "to that above" at the end, after everyone else had finished. I always guessed my son led those awful renditions, although I could never prove it. I do know that sniggers came from that same group as the congregation sang "The Old Rugged Cross," particularly at the phrase "the cross I'd gladly bear." The sniggerers were absolutely sure that the congregation had sung about "the cross-eyed gladly bear," and delighted in telling everyone.

Doubtlessly—without the help of mischievous youths—the new Israel worshiped by singing hymns, much as the old Israel had sung the Psalms. The Gospel of Luke is thought to contain portions of hymns the church sang. Examples are found 2:23–25 and 2:29–32. Thus, Simeon's prayer at the birth of Jesus is thought to have been sung by the church in worship. They joined with Simeon, expressing the great difference God makes when his presence in life is acknowledged. Perhaps you would like to join both Simeon and the early church now in seeking the peace they found in such acknowledgement. The words of the hymn are:

> Lord, now lettest thou thy servant
> depart in peace
> according to thy word,
> for my eyes have seen the
> salvation which thou hast prepared
> in the presence of all peoples, ... (2:29–31).

Peace be with you.

LUKE

Tradition assigns the name of Luke to this Gospel. It is Luke, the beloved physician and companion of Paul, who is suggested. Word studies of medical language in the book do not necessarily indicate a physician. However, in contrast to the account in Mark, the language used to describe "the woman with the issue of blood" seems to go out of its way to defend the role of the physician, possibly indicating a physician writer (compare Luke 8:43–48 to Mark 5:25–34).

Luke begins his Gospel with a prologue. In this introduction, he tells the reader why he is writing. He explains that although others have written, he intends to set forth a full and orderly account.

There are some clues as to the time of his writing. He used Mark, but not Matthew, causing some scholars to assume he wrote about the time of Matthew. Moreover, Luke wrote a second volume, Acts, dated about 90 A.D. It follows the Gospel. Luke's time frame of 70 A.D. (with his use of Mark) and 90 A.D. (with the writing of Acts) makes the date of 80–85 A.D. for the Gospel plausible.

Luke begins this relatively long book with the account of the births of John the Baptist and Jesus. Of the four Gospels, Luke and Matthew are the only writers who include the birth of Jesus at the beginning of their works. Luke is apparently also interested in showing that Christianity is not subversive. Operating without a legal acceptance by the state and coming under suspicion and local persecution, Luke stressed Jesus' political loyalty, Pilate's assurance of Jesus' innocence, and Herod Antipas's failure to find legal grounds for Jesus' death. Moreover, Luke seems bent on showing that Christianity is devoid of racial prejudice. He traces the genealogy of Jesus back to Adam, the father of the human race; a Samaritan becomes the hero of a parable; references to the strictly Jewish mission of Jesus are absent; and Luke alone records the mission charge to the "seventy," a traditional number for all the nations of the earth. Finally, the author shows a special interest in the poor, women, the hymns of the early church, the perils of wealth, prayer, miracles, and the Spirit.

Once again, in finding the continuity of the story from Genesis through Luke, and by understanding how the books are joined together, the Gospel of Luke continues the Covenant concept of the Old Testament, the Covenant now being made with God through Jesus. The Exodus concept underlies the story, as the follower journeys out of himself or herself and into the promised presence of God.

"This is the day which the Lord has made, let us rejoice and be glad in it."
Psalm 118:24

Chapter Forty-One

Present Blessings

Seminary can produce surprises. One surprise is the striking difference in religious viewpoints that students can hold. This was nowhere quite so clear to me as when I saw a seminary student with a full-blown futuristic religious perspective standing side by side with one whose religious viewpoint was almost entirely grounded in the present.

One of the characteristics of the Gospel of John is an interest in living the gospel in the present. The fourth Gospel, therefore, describes items that are usually projected into the future as being present realities. Scholars sometimes refer to this characteristic as realized eschatology. This means that John takes such concepts as judgment and eternal life and moves them into the present. Through faith, eternal life has already begun in the present.

This means that a person is already being judged by his or her choice and continuing choices. It is almost as though the writer does not want his readers to miss the realities of their faith by relegating them entirely to the future. Without saying it in so many words, he does not want them to be so caught up in a heavenly future that they are no earthly good now.

Today, we may remind ourselves that the "pie in the sky, by and by" may be delightful, but eating today's bread can be equally satisfying. Thus, John reminds us to live out our faith.

May good things be yours today as you contemplate the present blessings of your faith.

JOHN

Like the other Gospel writers, John's Gospel continues the story begun in Genesis. However, his book differs so much from the other Gospels that early in its history, it was spoken of as a theological Gospel. The assumption was that the other three Gospels were not theological. Today the assumption is more likely that all four writers wrote from a theological perspective.

John has some obvious differences from Matthew, Mark, and Luke. John features long discourses in his Gospel, whereas the other gospels show Jesus speaking in parables and short proverbial statements. Moreover, missing in John's Gospel are the birth narrative, baptism, and temptation of Jesus, as well as the Lord's Prayer, the institution of the Lord's Supper, and the agony in Gethsemane, among other features.

Introduced by a hymn to the Word (*logos*), the author goes back to the beginning of all things to introduce the Christ of his Gospel. John writes, "He was in the beginning . . ." (John 1:2). It is this preexistent, all-knowing One that is pictured. Even at his arrest, he calmly steps forward to be arrested, without the need to show Judas as betrayer. It is this Christ who moves through the crucifixion, ever in command. He promises the Paraclete or Comforter to continue to care for his flock after his death. The link to the preceding material in the Bible can be seen here. This book takes us all the way back to Genesis. If God created in the beginning, then the same God strides across John's Gospel as the Christ who is continuing the story.

John the Apostle links the present to the past in a unique fashion and presents to the reader a fourth portrait of Jesus.

> "Why are you cast down, O my soul, and why are you disquieted within me? Hope in God; for I shall again praise him, my help and my God."
> Psalm 43:5–6

Chapter Forty-Two
THE MIRACLE OF HOPE

The crowd of 66,782 fans was stunned. Just a few weeks before, they had been voted the best and loudest fans in the NFL. Suddenly they had been silenced. The Buffalo Bills had kicked a field goal with sixteen seconds left in the game. With a sixteen to fifteen score, it was over. The play-off game had been lost. Or so it seemed. On the ensuing kickoff, however, Lorenzo Neal fielded the ball, handed off to Frank Wycheck, who ran to the right, pulling the Buffalo defense in his direction. Turning, he threw a lateral to Kevin Dyson on the far left side of the field. The speedy Dyson, with an escort of Tennessee Titan blockers, ran untouched for 75 yards, making the winning touchdown. Dramatically, Nashville had triumphed over Buffalo. The crowd erupted in celebration at what was called "The Music City Miracle."

The Book of Acts begins after the disciples had been devastated by the crucifixion. They stood stunned by defeat. Or so it seemed. But it was all overturned by the dramatic reality of the resurrected Christ. The church emerged victorious.

Translated into the commonplaces of everyday life, the experience of Acts doesn't necessarily suggest victory out of every defeat for us. But it should cause us to approach everyday experiences with a passion for life. Hope and expectancy can generate that passion.

ACTS

If the experience at Mt. Sinai in the book of Exodus marked the beginning of the People of the Covenant, the experience of the resurrected Christ in the books of Acts marked the beginning of the church, the People of the New Covenant. Tying together the story of the Bible at this point shows the themes of covenant and Exodus extending right into the book of Acts. The People of the New Covenant make their own Exodus in the beginning of the church.

The book is the second of two volumes by the author of the Gospel of Luke. In addition to using the same style and vocabulary as Luke, the writer makes it clear in the beginning of Acts that this is true. Addressing the "most excellent Theophilus," whom he also addressed in the opening of Luke, he writes, "In the first book, O Theophilus, I have dealt with all that Jesus began to do and teach, until the day when he was taken up, . . ." (Acts 1:1). He then proceeds to tell the reader what followed in the experience of the People of the New Covenant.

Acts is the beginning of the history of the church. It is church history designed to lead readers to commit to the faith that had been set forth in Luke's Gospel. The book roughly divides itself into two sections. The first twelve chapters basically feature the Apostle Peter and the church. Chapter thirteen through the conclusion of the book sets forth the growth of the church through the work of the missionary Paul. The story of the church is basically the story of how it moves west. Beginning at Jerusalem, it is shown setting down roots in Asia Minor and eventually making a home in Rome, the capital of the Roman Empire. These beginnings of the church prepare the reader for a continued history that is set forth in the various letters or epistles of the New Testament.

> "He who through faith is righteous shall live."
> Romans 1:16

Chapter Forty-Three

A Determined Decision

The dentist looked at five-year-old Robby's tooth. He commented, "Nothing will happen for six months unless he fools with it." Robby made a determined decision. He wiggled his tooth regularly. It became a passion with him throughout the day to wiggle the tooth. At school, he allowed a fourth grader to push the tooth back as far as it would go. Hanging by a thread, his teacher pulled it. Taking his tooth home, Robby announced to his mother, "This was the best day of my life." Robby's constant wiggling of the tooth paid off in the prize that was placed under his pillow that night.

For many of us, having a tooth pulled doesn't constitute the best day of our lives. However, the constant steps that led Robby to make that comment may also help us. In the realm of the spirit, faith is a determined decision. It is a commitment that becomes a passion. Walking in the teachings of Jesus does not guarantee success. It does not promise any exemptions from life's hurts. It is not an escape from life. But the passion to walk through life by faith can set us straight on life's road. It may lead us to say, "This is the best day of my life." For "He who through faith is righteous shall live" (Rom. 1:16–17).

ROMANS

The first building block of our story in the New Testament is made up of the Gospels. The second is made up of history—the book of Acts. The letters or epistles make up the third building block. These letters are primarily from Paul to the churches. There are a few others from various authors. Together they continue the account of a people who began their covenant existence at Sinai, pushed through to settle in Canaan, and worked their way through the Dark Ages, kings, prophets, defeats, and an exile to finally return home, setting the stage for beginning again. The Gospels introduce Jesus the Christ. Acts chronicles the church that was built around him. The letters carry the story forward.

In Romans, Paul apparently introduces himself to the church in Rome. The letter comes as close to being a theological treatise as any of his letters. However, it too is a "bread and butter" message to a church, in which practical matters are addressed. It shares this characteristic with all of Paul's other letters. In them, he explains his understanding of the gospel.

The theme of the letter is found in Romans 1:16–17: "For in it [the gospel], the righteousness of God is revealed through faith for faith; as it is written, 'He who through faith is righteous shall live.'" It is a theme, like Exodus and Covenant, coming out of the Old Testament. It echoes Habakkuk 2:4, once again binding together the material we are considering into a continuous story. Paul presents the theme as the opportunity for a person to be made righteous out of his or her distorted spiritual position. He or she can be set straight and made right by exercising his or her faith and walking in it. All people are in need of this faith, and it is offered to all.

Paul briefly discusses the place of the Jewish nation in the continuing story and ends with various ethical teachings.

"God is our refuge and strength, a very present help in trouble.
Therefore we will not fear, though the earth should change,
though the mountains shake in the heart of the sea; . . ."
Psalm 46:1–2

Chapter Forty-Four

TROUBLES ABOUND

The words to a tune from the forties say: "The music goes round and round . . ." In the same way, the troubles of life seem to repeat themselves. We make the same complaints, get ourselves into the same predicaments, or watch as the ceiling falls in at the same place. Or so it seems. How good it would be if life would shape up the way we imagined it would as a child. "As soon as I get a bicycle, life will be smooth sailing the rest of the way," we imagined. But it hasn't been smooth sailing. Troubles abound. Is there no end to the cycle of our problems? Apparently not. To use the words of Job 5:7, ". . . man is born to trouble as the sparks [of a fire] fly upward."

However, there is a different element in the constant cycle of happenings that occured in first century and still occur in the twenty-first. There is another line in that forties tune that says, "And it comes out here." If we follow the trumpet's note from the mouthpiece to its exit, we know it comes out at the bell of the instrument. How we plan to blow into the mouthpiece of life's trumpet determines to a great extent where the problems "come out." We cannot shape life to our desires, of course, even if we get the bicycle we so desperately wanted. But we can determine to try to face life's troubles. We can trust in God for the ultimate outcome. We can purse our lips and daily blow into the trumpet of life the most beautiful music we can manage.

May your strength be more than equal to your troubles today, as you determine to make music out of your life.

1 CORINTHIANS

The Pentatuech told us of various problems arising in the early experiences of the People of the Covenant—the people regretted leaving Egypt, they complained to Moses that there was not enough food and water, and they argued about his leadership, among other things. 1 Corinthians describes problems arising in the early experience of the church at Corinth. The link between the present story and the preceding story continues, although it is an unfortunate link at this point. Among the various problems 1 Corinthians describes are divisions in the church, incest, lawsuits among the members, and the pursuit of knowledge that produces superior feelings.

Paul established the church at Corinth and spent about eighteen months there. After leaving, he was visited by a group from the church, asking for his help with problems in the church. Later, he received a letter from the church, once again asking for help with particular questions. The book of 1 Corinthians addresses these very practical issues and others in the early life of the church. In a particular situation at Corinth, the book unfolds the history of the church in the first century, much as does Acts.

It is interesting that the issues the church found challenging then have made their way into the modern church—issues such as women in worship, speaking in tongues, the Lord's Supper, and the resurrection, among others. As the writers of the Old Testament gave expression to diverse answers, so the church has given diverse answers to these and other issues. What unifies the problems and answers to these questions from both People of the Covenant in the Old Testament and People of the New Covenant in the New Testament is the faith that both have in a common God and a common goal.

> "My grace is sufficient for you, for my power is made perfect in weakness."
> 2 Corinthians 12:9

Chapter Forty-Five

SUFFICIENT GRACE

Two sisters, Loretta Robinson and Vera Vaughn, clean our condo. They do it well. Sometimes they combine good work with great fun. Last January, I came home to an unexpected display that they had left just inside the front door. There I found a black plastic garbage bag, neatly flattened out on the throw rug. On it were very old and very battered deck shoes. They had been rescued that day from the snow. For months, I had left the shoes on the back deck, after working in the yard. They had suffered through blistering heat, hail, rain, sleet, and snow. They were grotesquely curled up at the toes and badly separated at the soles. The sisters thought they had suffered enough. They left me a large, white, printed note, propped up as though advertising a sale. It read, "Do you really think you can rescue these bad boys? Don't you think we should just take them into the woods and shoot them?" I had to agree and left them a note the following week to that effect.

Perhaps we have a few years under our belt, or for some other reason the experiences of life have left us a little frayed around the edges. It may be that someone thinks we should be taken into the woods. In fact, a wise-cracking friend I had not seen in a long time thought so in my case. Running into him as we left a restaurant, he blurted out, "Hey friend, I thought you were dead." I'm not sure he didn't continue thinking that even as I looked the rascal in the eyes.

Paul found life intense. He had been pushed down to the depths and was gasping for breath. But he was not ready for the woods. He was ready for life. He declared as much in 2 Corinthians. God said to him, "My grace is sufficient for you, for my power is made perfect in weakness" (2 Cor. 12:9).

Is life curling up? Is your soul feeling separated? Now may be the best time to seize the moment. Have you watched a sunrise lately? Appreciated loved ones? Read in a quiet corner? Said a prayer that consists only of things for which you are thankful? Told someone that you love her or him? Visited someone who would welcome a visit? Forgiven someone? Forgiven yourself? The grace of God is sufficient for us. We're not ready for the woods!

2 CORINTHIANS

2 Corinthians may be more than a single letter from Paul to his church at Corinth. In fact, scholars think this writing may conserve portions of two letters.

The second communication is very personal. In it, Paul has apparently been criticized. As he writes, Paul does something he does not ordinarily do. He defends himself.

The tone of the writing in chapters 10–13 is rather sharp. Some scholars believe these chapters are part of a separate letter the apostle sent to the church. He is answering his critics. An example of the criticism and reply is found in 10:10–11: "For they say, 'His letters are weighty and strong, but his bodily presence is weak, and his speech of no account.' Let such people understand that what we say by letter when absent, we do when present." He justifies himself, speaking uncharacteristically in an almost boasting manner, and he even relates his sufferings as an apostle.

In contrast, chapters 1–9 have a calm tone. Having heard that the dissenting church members have had a change of heart toward him, Paul writes a conciliatory letter. It speaks of working together and of comfort. Thus, grace has been sufficient.

One item that gets special attention in this section is the offering being taken for the poor saints in Jerusalem. Paul asks that the church complete the offering so that it may be sent on its way.

In conclusion, it is interesting to note that 1 Corinthians sets forth issues in the early church much like Exodus did early in the experience of the people of the covenant. Then 2 Corinthians records complaints against Paul, much like the Pentateuch sets forth complaints against Moses. Thus the story of the new covenant continues to unfold, revealing similarities to the story that has preceded it.

> [Philip questioned a reader of Isaiah] "Do you understand what you are reading?" And he said, "How can I, unless someone guides me?"
> Acts 8:30–31

Chapter Forty-Six
APPRECIATING GUIDES

When Paul spoke of the person he had become in the faith, it was necessary for him to reexamine who he had been. This exercise is valuable for each of us. Who are we? Rather than easily giving our name in response, the question may require reexamining who we have been. That in turn may lead us to those who have been guides along the way to making us who we now are.

It shouldn't be difficult for us to remember our guides. Have there been mothers, fathers, pastors, Sunday School teachers, scout leaders, teachers, civic leaders, and others who have helped make us who we are? To a great extent we are the sum of their guidance. That is who we are.

That being the case, is it not proper that we identify and appreciate ours guides? A note, a phone call, a visit, or an e-mail to a guide may be the best action we can take today.

GALATIANS

Galatians is a link in the story that began at Sinai. The covenant experience with God continues. However, Galatians represents change in the story also. The covenant has emphasized strict adherence to the law of the Old Testament. Facing the challenge of Gentiles or non-Jews committing to the covenant, Galatians dramatically breaks the link. Paul proclaims Christian liberty at this point. For example, freedom from being circumcised and from the food laws are a part of that freedom. Although the ties to the early story continue, the necessity of a non-Jew having to assume all the requirements of Judaism before entering the church are abolished.

This assertion of freedom did not go unchallenged. The struggle between Paul and those who denied this liberty dominated much of the course of history from the mid-fifties through several following decades. In the end, Paul and the proponents of liberty won the battle. The church became characterized by such liberty.

It was a hard-fought battle. The anti-liberty forces, referred to as Judaizers, followed Paul about and denied his assertions. Others, sometimes referred to as Gnostics or libertines, misunderstood or twisted Paul's work in Galatians to mean that liberty for the Christian was to do anything he or she pleased.

Weathering the storm, the understanding emerged in the continuing story of the covenant that faith surpassed and replaced law as a way of righteous living for Jew and non-Jew. The righteous live by faith.

In arriving at the above conclusion, Paul was compelled to make sense out of his own personal life, which had previously been spent living by the law. He dealt with the problem by looking upon the law as a guide that led him to Christ. He concluded that the law cannot give life. Rather, its purpose is to lead to the Christ who can give life.

The book of Galatians is a monumental stepping stone in the story of faith.

"Therefore be imitators of God, as beloved children. And walk
in love, as Christ loved us and gave himself for us . . ."
Ephesians 5:1

Chapter Forty-Seven
RESPONSIBLE RELATIONSHIPS

In an interview, the former slave recalled worship services on the plantation. "You always knew the preacher would take his text from Ephesians," she related. The text she was referring to is "Slaves, be obedient to those who are your earthly masters, with fear and trembling in singleness of heart, as to Christ" (Eph. 6:5).

In reading such passages in the Bible, it is clear that the church did not launch an all-out offensive against the institution of slavery in the first century. There may have been several reasons. The Roman Empire would have surely crucified the church's effort. In Ephesians, the author may have thought the impending return of Christ would make a campaign unnecessary. Or the thought may have been that converting the world to the gospel would in itself eliminate slavery. But this and similar passages in the Bible have led some readers through the years to defend slavery. This seems strange. The movement that furnishes the foundation for the Bible story we are following is the Exodus. And the Exodus is a deliverance of the people from slavery, of course.

Having said this, the text the preacher used in speaking to the slaves has a companion. The companion text is "Masters, do the same to them, and forbear threatening, knowing that he who is both their Master and yours is in heaven, and that there is no partiality with him" (Eph. 6:9). In each case the parties are called to responsible relationships. Husbands are to be responsible in relationships with their wives. In turn, wives are to be responsible in relationships with their husbands. The same thing is true of parents to children and children to parents. Moreover, the relationships are to be carried out as though they are done to and for Christ.

Perhaps there is a troublesome relationship that could use fine-tuning today. Ephesians suggests applying personal responsibility in the relationship and carrying it out as though it is being done to Christ himself. May grace, strength, and success be yours in the effort.

EPHESIANS

Ephesians may have appeared close to the end of the first century. The debate over the manner in which non-Jews were to be received into the church had diminished. Echoes of Ruth and Jonah's Old Testament arguments for including non-Jews among the people of God had long ago ceased to be needed. The manner in which non-Jews were to become the people of God seems to have been dealt with as well. This mid-century topic of discussion characterized earlier letters.

If the absence of the debate, which is at the heart of Galatians and early Pauline writings, is not a factor in determining the date, then Paul is thought to have written it as one of his Prison Epistles, along with Philemon, Philippians, and Colossians.

Unlike letters which speak of the local church, Ephesians speaks of the universal church and of the redeemed drawn from various backgrounds and nationalities to form the body of Christ or the church.

Because the letter contains no personal references or "local color," it is often thought to be an encyclical letter, used to accompany a group of Paul's letters and meant for all the churches.

The book is divided into two main parts. The first is a discussion of God's intention—from the foundation of the world—to bring all men together in one body, the universal church (Eph. 1:1–3:21). The second division (Eph. 4:1–6:20) is devoted to various ethical expectations that are to characterize the church.

The most famous passage of the book is a picture of Christ's followers armed like Roman soldiers as they are sent to do battle with evil (Eph. 6:10–20).

> "I can endure all things in him who strengthens me."
> Philippians 4:13

Chapter Forty-Eight
LOOKING UP

There is a story of a prisoner whose cell had but one small window. It was at ground level. Looking out, someone else might have noticed trash that had been thrown upon the dirt, or mud made by the dirt when it rained, or dust swirling about, blown by dry wind. It was a drab view. This prisoner, however, saw something else. He saw blue sky, drifting clouds, and the sun by day. At night, he saw the moon and the stars. There was one reason he could do this. At the little window, he just didn't look out, he looked up.

In prison, Paul wrote a famous passage that is recorded in Philippians. He wrote, "I can do [endure] all things in him who strengthens me" (Phil. 4:13).

Life often demands sheer endurance. Our call to "do" all things is actually a call to "endure." The challenge can be seen in a hospital, an office building, an assembly line, a nursing home, in various situations—in our own situation. Sometimes our hands are tied, and the only thing to do is to endure. Paul's counsel in such times is to "look up." Through Christ, Paul endured victoriously. Perhaps the joy of this day is to be found in similar endurance.

PHILIPPIANS

Although Ephesians was probably written later in the century, if one assumed an earlier date for Ephesians, there would be four letters called Prison Letters. Paul would have written Ephesians, Philippians, Colossians, and Philemon while in prison. Tradition assumes that he was in prison in Rome, although Caesarea or Ephesus have also been suggested as the possible site of imprisonment.

Apparently, Paul maintained a close and happy relationship with the church at Philippi, the first church he had established in Europe. While awaiting trial, the church ministered to Paul as he had always ministered to the church. They sent a gift to him by Epaphroditus. In response, Paul wrote to thank them for the gift and their care. He brings them up to date on his life in prison and shares with them guidance about various matters.

The letter is characterized by joy. Paul's attitude toward life continues to be marked by this quality, even though he is in prison and faces possible death. The theme of joy overrides all else.

One of my two purposes for writing this book is to show how the parts of the Bible relate to the whole. It has been my intention not to picture isolated bits and pieces, but to give a complete overview. In this regard, the book of Philippians continues a theme of the Exodus, the joy of freedom. It is a joy that is found in a covenant between God and the people at Sinai, carried into the land of promise, lost for a while during the Dark Ages, found again during the monarchy under David, clung to during the fall of the kingdoms and an Exile, but then renewed on a return to Palestine from exile. It was given a new life in the New Covenant under Jesus, about whom the Gospels and Acts have spoken and the letters now speak. In Philippians, Paul announces that joy once again.

> "The earth is the Lord's and the fullness thereof, the world and those who dwell therein, for he has founded it upon the seas, and established it upon the rivers."
> Psalm 24:1–2

Chapter Forty-Nine

COSMIC GLUE

Many years ago, the hardware department of the J. P. Morris General Store featured a special display and a challenge. The display consisted of two short pieces of rounded two by twos. Each would fit nicely into the grip of your hand. The two pieces of lumber had been glued together with a new product the store was selling. A prize was offered to anyone who could successfully break apart the two pieces with their hands. Many tried. To my knowledge, no one was able to separate the two.

A theme that is played majestically throughout the book of Colossians is that Christ is the binding power that holds the moon, the stars, the planets, and the very universe together. But this cosmic bond extends to humanity as well. He has the ability to hold life together. He is sufficient.

More times than we like, life seems destined to break into pieces. This appears to surface in the very nature of things from time to time. We feel fragmented, and we yearn for wholeness. Is there something or someone to pull us together? The answer Colossians offers is reassuring. A prayerful identification of the fragments and a quiet surrender of each fragment to God is the assurance. The Eternal God can supply the bond to restore our sense of wholeness. The God who created life is the same God who is always there to help us pull the pieces together each time they fall apart. That is our reminder. We need look no further for the bond we seek.

COLOSSIANS

Including this writing in the Prison Letters would have called for an earlier date than was probably true of the letter. In any case, the letter was written to discourage a kind of syncretistic religion which fused bits and pieces from various religions into one entity. Seeking help in their lives, people in the town of Colossae may have taken a little Judaism and a little astrology, and mixed it with a strange religious conglomerate called Gnosticism to form a single faith. It was an unnecessary mixture, based upon judgments from various quarters. Thus the author of Colossians wrote, "Therefore let no one pass judgment on you in questions of food and drink or with regard to a festival or a new moon or a sabbath" (Col. 2:16). "Let no one disqualify you, insisting on self-abasement and worship of angels taking his stand on visions, puffed up without reason by his sensuous mind..." (Col. 2:18). And, "If with Christ you died to the elemental spirits of the universe, why do you live as if you still belonged to the world?" (Col. 2:20).

In an environment of wavering loyalties to mixed religious ingredients, the author calls the church at Colossae back to a worship of Christ alone. He had the power they needed to heal the problems of their disjointed lives. They need not search for another.

> "Rejoice always, pray constantly, give thanks in all circumstances,
> for this is the will of God in Christ Jesus for you."
> 1 Thessalonians

Chapter Fifty

RESILIENCE IN FAITH

Having been sent by Paul to check on the struggling church at Thessalonica, it must have been a pleasant surprise to Timothy to find the young church continuing in its faith. The threat to its existence had been faced, and the church was surviving. The fact that it was young and immature had not prevented its survival.

The afflictions of life in the form of neglect, prejudice, abuse, poverty, jealously, discrimination, unkindness, or a multitude of other afflictions, seem particularly damaging to the young and immature. That they can overcome these challenges may be surprising, although the resilience of a youthful faith may be at the heart of their survival.

In fact, the older and more mature in faith may be equally at risk in face of life's afflictions. Moreover, like an old rubber band, they may have lost their ability to spring back. Paul suggests that the source of resilience is faith. Resilience lies at the heart of faith for young and old. He advises, "Rejoice always, pray constantly, give thanks in all circumstances; for this is the will of God in Christ Jesus for you" (1 Thess. 5:16–18).

May Paul's suggestion be sufficient for your affliction.

1 THESSALONIANS

1 Thessalonians may have been the earliest of Paul's writings, unless that distinction goes to Galatians. The church at Thessalonica

was a young church that struggled after Paul's departure. The threat of persecution hovered over the church, and in Paul's case, a possible charge of treason may have necessitated his leaving prematurely.

Concerned for the immature church, Paul sent Timothy to give them assistance. On his return, Timothy brought word of their continued faith and loyalty. Paul then responded with his letter of appreciation for the church in which he offered hope and encouragement.

The theme of the letter is the return of Christ. There are two concerns that have arisen in regard to the return. The first is a concern for loved ones who die before the return. Paul assures them that the dead will precede even those who are alive at the time into the Lord's presence (1 Thess. 4:13–18). The second is a question about the time of the return. He reminds them that the time is unknown. "The Lord will come like a thief in the night" (1 Thess. 5:2).

Paul then concludes the letter with various moral and ethical instructions.

"Drink water from your own cistern, flowing water
from your own well."
Proverbs 5:15

Chapter Fifty-One

No Freeloaders

It was hard to tell whether the crane was real or not. He sat motionless on the highest point of the beachfront restaurant's cupola. It was only by looking at two other cranes, who were sitting absolutely still atop tall light fixtures in the parking lot, that you could guess that all of the cranes were not fixtures, but were really alive. The cranes contrasted sharply with several seagulls that were flying, soaring, and dipping, busily hunting their food. The contrast between the two groups was striking.

At one time, before the advent of the coastal restaurants, the cranes, like the gulls, had busily worked for their food. But now they no longer hunted. They had learned to beg instead. They became "freeloaders," dependent upon the generosity of restaurant guests and cooks.

Expecting the return of the Messiah, some folks in Thessalonica allowed their expectancy to drift into laziness and became "freeloaders" in the community. Paul's answer to the problem was a simple one. If one does not work, then he should not eat.

Expectancy is not a do-nothing state of mind. On the contrary, it is more than ever a "do what I can, where I am, with what I have, for Jesus' sake," state of mind. May your expectancy be blessed with such a rewarding state of mind.

2 THESSALONIANS

2 Thessalonians is much like 1 Thessalonians in language. It is almost a reproduction in places. Moreover, the theme is the same in both letters: the return of Christ. This has caused some students of the New Testament to believe that Paul would not have repeated himself on the same subject. Some guess that another must therefore have written 2 Thessalonians in Paul's name. Others believe that shifting the order of the books gives a better flow to understanding why the author treats the same subject twice.

The general consensus is that Paul wrote both letters. The reason that he wrote them on the same subject had to do with the questions that he had been asked. In the first letter, the concerns the people voiced were about loved ones who had died before the return had taken place. They were also concerned about when the return was to take place. Paul addressed those two issues in discussing the return, each in a different letter.

In 2 Thessalonians, the problem was different. Apparently enough time had passed since the ascent of Christ that some followers had gotten careless about their work and daily activities. They had quit their jobs and were doing nothing. In the process, they had become dependent upon others who were conscientious and who were living responsible lives as they awaited the return. It is this issue that arises and makes a second letter from Paul necessary. 2 Thessalonians addresses the issue.

> "Fight the good fight of the faith, take hold of the eternal life to which you were called when you made the good confession in the presence of many witnesses."
> 1 Timothy 6:12

Chapter Fifty-Two
OFFENSE FOR LIFE'S BLOWS

Many years ago, under Coach Paul Dietzel, the Louisiana State University football team had a special defensive unit. When the opponent seemed to be getting the upper hand, the band played a tinkling Chinese tune. Eleven men called the Chinese Bandits were sent in. More often than not, this defensive unit turned back the surging opponent.

About the time of 1 Timothy, the church faced community pressures, internal problems, and a growing threat of persecution by Rome. The temptation was to turn to a special defense. However, examining Paul in Galatians, his best defense in facing life's threat was a shining offense. In the Spirit, he walked in his faith. He continued to do the things that gave a positive expression to his faith.

My lifelong friend Arlen Blackwell is experiencing a serious illness. It is interesting to observe that he has not chosen to retreat from life in an attempt to defend against his foe. Rather, he continues to share his faith. He continues to help others. He continues to give himself to life. When asked about himself, he says simply, "I'm all right."

Life threatens in a ceaseless variety of ways. Like Paul, our best defense is a flourishing offense of our faith. Therefore, ". . . aim at righteousness, godliness, faith, love, and steadfastness. Fight the good fight of the faith; take hold of eternal life to which you were called when you made the good confession in the presence of many witnesses" (6:11b–12).

1 TIMOTHY

1 Timothy is one of three books (1 and 2 Timothy and Titus) referred to as the Pastoral Letters. In them, the pastor offers counsel to his flock, the church. Tradition suggests that Paul was released from prison in Rome, traveled to Crete, and was arrested a final time. It is suggested that he wrote the Pastoral Letters there.

However, because the letters reflect conditions that existed long after Paul's day, lack Paul's characteristic ideas about faith and the Spirit, contain a different vocabulary and style, and assume a more developed church organization than what was current in Paul's generation, scholars believe the Pastorals were written later by a disciple of Paul.

This raises the question of pseudonymity, or the practice of writing letters in the name of a deceased person. This was not thought of as a forgery in the days of the early church, as it would be today. It was common at the time for a disciple to write a work to perpetuate the thoughts of his leader. He wrote as he believed the leader would have written at a later time. This was intended to honor the deceased, not to deceive the reader. Both Jews and early Christians produced a body of pseudonymous writings in the names of Moses, Noah, Thomas, Peter, and John, among others.

1 Timothy is written to a generation of believers to whom apostolic truths are entrusted. The believers are to defend doctrine against heresies. In addition to putting down false teachings, the church is given the qualifications to use in the selection of deacons and other church officers. The letter also deals with the role of women and slaves during that day.

> "God did not give us a spirit of timidity but a spirit of power and love and self control."
> 2 Timothy 1:7

Chapter Fifty-Three
DISABLED AND ENABLED

My wife was helping to temporarily care for a quadriplegic patient. He was lifted from his bed by a hydraulic lift and placed in a portable tub where he could be given a bath. Possessed by a calm voice and quiet behavior, the patient talked readily and easily with his caretakers. Apparently, he had long ago come to terms with the bullet that had caused his paralysis. When he requested to be carefully dressed to go to church, the reason he had accepted his condition so fully became clear. It was his faith. While others around him with far less disabling problems cursed their fate, he approached his life in a "spirit of power and love and self-control" (2 Timothy 1:7). He was a living example of the advice given to Timothy.

All of us have disabling problems of one kind or another. Perhaps now is a good time to be reminded of a sincere faith that can rekindle the gift of God that is within and enable us to live triumphantly through those problems. If that can happen—and 2 Timothy proclaims that it can—it calls for our finest investment in faith.

2 TIMOTHY

In the second of the Pastoral Letters, the teacher continues his instructions to his flock. They are to remember the faith that is within them and to be courageous in showing evidence of it in the world. The example of Paul is given to remind and encourage them (2 Tim. 1).

They are to maintain single-mindedness about their preaching and witnessing. They are to avoid "godless chatter" (2:16) and "disputing about words" (2:14), and they are to have nothing to do with "stupid, senseless controversies" (2:23). They are reminded that ". . . the Lord's servant must not be quarrelsome but kindly to every one, an apt teacher, forbearing, correcting his opponents with gentleness" (chapter 2).

Describing the days as days of stress, the hearers are to avoid people who are "lovers of self, lovers of money, proud, arrogant, abusive, disobedient to their parents, ungrateful, unholy, inhuman, implacable, slanderers, profligates, fierce, haters of good, treacherous, reckless, swollen with conceit, lovers of pleasure rather than lovers of God, holding the form of religion but denying the power of it" (2 Tim. 3:2–5).

At this point, we are put in touch with the theme that we have been following since Genesis. Without mentioning the covenant or Exodus as such, the reader is suddenly tied to all that has preceded him or her. The hearer is to be encouraged in his or her faith by recalling the past. "But as for you, continue in what you have learned and have firmly believed, knowing from whom you learned it and how from childhood you have been acquainted with the sacred writings [Old Covenant] which are able to instruct you [point you toward the Christ] for salvation through faith in Christ Jesus. All scripture is inspired by God and profitable for teaching, for reproof, for correction, and for training in righteousness, that the man of God may be complete, equipped for every good work" (3:14–17).

A crown of righteousness awaits Paul and all those who fight the good fight, finish the race, and keep the faith (chapter 4).

> "For freedom Christ has set us free; stand fast therefore, and
> do not submit again to a yoke of slavery."
> Galatians 5:1

Chapter Fifty-Four

THE SPIRIT AND THE LETTER

There was a professor of theology at the seminary who had escaped Germany just before Hitler shut the door on those who wished to leave. On one occasion, the professor was invited by a student to attend a tent revival meeting. Quizzed about whether or not he would attend, he replied that, like Paul, should the Spirit so move him, he would respond to an appropriate call and walk the sawdust trail at the meeting. He was ready to do so, regardless of whether or not all of the theological *i*'s had been dotted or theological *t*'s had been crossed. He was a man of the Spirit.

One of the striking differences between Paul's former life and his life after his conversion was that formerly he had lived by a code or set of rules, but after his conversion, he walked by the Spirit. The laws had only been a preparation for a more abundant life in the Spirit.

One of the temptations that sometimes surfaces in the church is the return to making decisions by the letter of the law rather than by following the Spirit. This backward move can tempt the church to become judgmental and even self-righteous. It can produce a rules-dominated mindset in place of a Spirit-filled mindset. Paul and the German theology professor chose the latter. The choice is clear.

TITUS

The Pastorals reflect a time when the church struggled internally to establish itself. The book of Titus focuses on the requirements for its leaders (such as elders in every town and bishops). The elder is to be blameless, a husband of one wife, and his children are to be "believers and not open to the charge of being profligate or insubordinate" (Titus 1:6).

The bishop is to be blameless and "not arrogant, quick-tempered, or a drunkard, violent or greedy for gain, but hospitable, a lover of goodness, master of himself, upright, holy, and self-controlled" (Titus 1:7–8). Little is said about the earlier emphasis in Paul's churches on the leader's charismatic gifts, ecstatic experiences of the Spirit, and prophetic speech—his walk in faith. Here the struggle is pictured as sorting out what the faith is, as opposed to what the faith is not.

The struggle is mirrored in the characterization of those who are "insubordinate men, empty talkers, and deceivers, especially the circumcision party" (Titus 1:10). These are pictured as corrupting the faith (chapter 1).

In light of the struggle, suggestions are then made to several groups in the church: older men, older women, younger men, and finally slaves (chapter 2).

The ongoing struggle that the church has with the world outside is also reflected in Titus. The church is to set a good example before the world of non-believers by behaving well toward rulers and authorities. The people of the church are to live exemplary lives of faith and ethical purity as heirs in hope of eternal life (chapter 3).

> "Formerly he was useless to you, but now he is indeed
> useful to you and to me."
> Philemon 11

Chapter Fifty-Five

TO BE USEFUL

I once heard about a mentally challenged young man. Every day, his family rolled his wheelchair to the front lawn. There he took upon himself the responsibility of greeting people driving to work. With a smile and a wave to each one, he gave the riders a good beginning to their day. It was a gift that he expected to give and that they equally expected to receive. He was a modern Onesimus. He made himself useful.

The need to be of use is not uncommon, of course. It seems to be part of the essence of life itself. We need a reason for being alive. By the same token, our usefulness may be beneficial to someone other than ourselves.

Usefulness today could mean a significant entry in a journal that might be read by another generation of the family. It could mean an endeavor to give a sour relationship a happier closure. May your faith lead you to examine appropriate avenues of usefulness, and open to you the joy of their pursuit.

PHILEMON

Philemon is the recipient of a personal letter from Paul. Paul is in prison. Thus the writing is one of the Prison Letters. Apparently under house arrest, Paul has received a runaway slave.

Paul has converted the slave, Onesimus, to the Christian faith. Then Paul persuades him to return to his master, Philemon. Philemon himself had been converted by Paul at an earlier time, and a Christian congregation was now meeting in his home. The law stated that slaves were meant to obey their masters. Paul is aware of this legality and the absolute authority Philemon has over his slave. But Paul asks the master to receive the slave back, not just as a slave, but as a Christian brother. In a play on words, using the slave's name, Paul writes that he once was not useful (Oneimus) to you, but now he is useful (Onesimus).

Paul is counting on the new relationship between the two to bring reconciliation. He does not try to force the issue with a command. In sending Onesimus back, he sends this tactful letter to his friend Philemon, hoping to guide the issue.

> "Hear my cry, O God, listen to my prayer; from the end of the earth I call to thee, when my heart is faint . . ."
> Psalm 61:1–2

Chapter Fifty-Six
RUNNING ON EMPTY

Have you ever owned a car whose gas gauge registered past the "F" mark when the tank was full? The car I had seemed to run an inordinately long time before reaching the half-tank mark. However, once it reached the halfway point, the indicator raced wildly toward empty. Driver beware! If I got anywhere near the "E" mark, no action short of a major infusion of gas would persuade it to budge. In contrast, my wife's car ran on empty by using gas fumes, or some other such magic. Not my old car.

Built like the latter, many try to move through life on empty. With credit cards maxed out, daily calendars overflowing, family members rarely seeing each other, and stress levels constantly mounting, life is chock full of everything but spirit to energize it. Like the natives carrying their head packs through the jungle, the time comes eventually to sit on the packs and wait for the spirit to catch up with the body. We are built for an infusion of the Spirit through meditation and worship. This is true whether in bed with an illness or barreling down the interstate. We cannot run on empty without exhaustion.

If members of the congregation in Hebrews were unsettled and longed for the past, it is likely they were running on empty. In view of that, the writer urged, "Forsake not the assembling of yourselves together as is the case with some" (Heb. 10:25).

The answer to their unsettled state was to return to meditation and worship. It is sound advice for a generation trying to run on gas fumes. Saying we don't have time to meditate and pray is like saying we don't have time to put gasoline in our car. The time taken to do so allows the mechanical vehicle, as well as the spiritual being, to function.

HEBREWS

Among the groups of writings in the New Testament, one is designated Hebrews and the General Letters. These writings may be so designated because they address general issues rather than specific problems, as many of Paul's letters did. Or they may have addressed the churches in general, rather than specific churches, as did many of the letters of Paul. The group consists of Hebrews, James, 1 Peter, 2 Peter, and Jude.

The author of the Book of Hebrews wrote at a time when some Jewish followers were entertaining the thought of leaving the church and returning to the fold of Judaism. The denial of one's faith is the subject of more than one passage in the book. Such a background may mirror post-Temple times, after the destruction of Jerusalem, when the distinction between church and synagogue became increasingly pronounced and an allegiance to one or the other group was magnified. The threat of persecution was hanging over the church, and enthusiasm for the church by some followers had become jaded, both of which prompted some to entertain the idea of abandoning the cause.

A primary argument in the first ten chapters of Hebrews asserts that Jesus is greater than any one of a succession of great figures (Moses, the angels, Melchizedek, etc.) in the Old Testament. Moreover, the reader is reminded that the contribution of Jesus in the New Covenant is superior to any contribution made under the Old Covenant. Apparently, the author aims to convince his readers that it is futile to consider a return to Judaism. Jesus and the New Covenant are obviously superior and therefore have the answer to man's needs. In the face of the waning enthusiasm and the threat of persecution, the writer encourages them to persevere in their discipleship, like the people of faith who had done so before them.

The book of Hebrews is usually spoken of as a letter. In some respects, it doesn't resemble a letter, however. There is no salutation. The greeting to the readers is absent, as is a commendation of their effort to fulfill their discipleship. Although it closes like a letter, lack of full resemblance to a letter may suggest that it originally was a sermon that has been given letter-like qualities. Like a sermon, it continually develops its theme, uses "speaker" terminology, and closes with a section of exhortation, much like a sermon might.

> "For the needy shall not always be forgotten, and the hope of
> the poor shall not perish for ever."
> Psalm 9:18

Chapter Fifty-Seven

RAGS, RICHES, AND RELIGION

The arthritic, partly balding, red-haired man slowly worked his way out of an old pickup truck parked in front of the bank. The truck was battered and worn from years of use. The same might have been said about its driver. He wore a rumpled khaki shirt, slightly soiled work pants, and old scuffed shoes. An aged straw hat shaded his sunburned face. He was a picture of a man down on his luck. So clear was the picture to one young, kindhearted girl that she went into nearby stores to collect money for the old man. In soliciting contributions, she received a surprise. She learned that the old gentleman actually had sufficient funds to buy the bank. His battered truck and worn-out clothes had deceived her.

Our "rags" seem to identify us. In the Old Testament, there is an understanding implying that one who is wealthy is also righteous. One of the clues to Job's righteousness was his wealth. The backside of the understanding was that poverty meant unrighteousness. So one could identify a man by his "rags" or lack of them.

Such thought may or may not be challenged by the book of James. But the book seems caught up in taking to task those who applaud the rich and overlook the poor. Wealth may not be wrong per se, and poverty certainly may not be good, but to make distinctions in the church because a person falls into the latter category is decidedly wrong. James reminds his readers, "For if a man with gold rings and in fine clothing comes into your assembly, and a poor man in shabby clothing also comes in, and you pay attention to the one who wears the fine clothing and say, 'Have a seat here, please,' while you say to the poor man 'Stand there,' or 'sit at my feet,' have you not made distinctions among yourselves, and become judges with evil thoughts?" (James 2:2–4).

Aside from the injustice of prejudging a person by his or her clothes, the opportunity of knowing the real person may be missed. In undertaking to know the person beneath the "rags," may we experience the delightful surprise of the kindhearted girl who asked for an offering for a poorly dressed old man.

JAMES

James is much like an Old Testament book. It is a book of ethical instructions with which the prophets would have felt at home. Aside from its obvious Christ-centered passages, it might pass as an Old Testament book.

If in fact James, the brother of Jesus, is the author, it may have been written about 40–60 A.D. James died in 62 A.D. If some other James wrote it, perhaps it was written between 80–90 A.D., or after the time of Paul. This later date is suggested because of James's treatment of the faith-works controversy. Paul wrote about faith and works in the context of how one secured salvation. James seems to write about the relationship after salvation has been obtained. It is difficult to date James because its short, imperative ethical exhortations come from a variety of backgrounds. Perhaps the later date is to be preferred.

The story line of James does not develop a central theme with related subthemes emerging along the way. Instead, it moves from its first statement to the last in a kind of haphazard fashion. Sometimes a subject is taken up, dropped, and then abruptly taken up at another point in a different context.

Some of the admonitions of James are: life's trials (1:1–4), asking for wisdom (1:5–8), temptation (1:12–15), God, author of good (1:16–18), anger (1:19–21), doing the Word (1:22–25), pure religion (1:26–27), partiality (2:1–13), faith and works (2:14–26), the tongue (3:1–12), wisdom (3:13–18), fighting and wars (4:1–10), judging (4:11–12), the future (4:13–17), storing up riches (5:1–6), coming of the lord (5:7–11), mutual trust (5:12), help in various conditions (5:13–18), and returning to the Truth (5:19–20).

> "For as the heavens are high above the earth, so great is his steadfast love toward those who fear him; as far as the east is from the west, so far does he remove our transgressions from us."
> Psalm 103:11

Chapter Fifty-Eight
GRACE AND BLAME

Blaming one's self may not seem to belong to the category of persecution. It is not totalitarian persecution or community persecution. But it does qualify as such to one who inflicts self-blame upon his inner person, after it has already been rooted out and discarded. It is self-persecution in the form of reopening old wounds, reliving old hurts, fighting old battles, and revisiting old mistakes. We may have little control over other forms of persecution, but we do not have to submit ourselves to a self-persecution of this sort.

The main reason for this is not found within an arsenal of self-helps, which may or may not rescue us. The real reason is found in grace—the eraser of ills that God freely offers. That is not to say that we will not find ourselves meeting old ills unexpectedly and unwillingly. It happens. Reminders flash up in our consciousness. But the quiet reminder that overcomes all others is the reminder that what we couldn't do for ourselves in the struggle with those ills, God has erased through grace—his unmerited favor. After admission, submission, and forgiveness, it is unnecessary to resurrect self-blame again. Grace makes it so. "That word is the good news that was preached to you" (1 Pet. 1:25). Why not remember that and make a fresh start?

1 PETER

Some scholars suggest the writing is pseudonymous because of its style and vocabulary. Moreover, they say the writer's expertise in dealing with the Greek version of the Old Testament, the Septuagint, does not reflect the knowledge of someone who practiced the law before his conversion. It reflects a literary skill. Such thought would suggest an author other than a Palestine fisherman, they argue.

Be that as it may, the aim of the writing seems clear. Located in 1 Peter 5:12, is the exhortation to "stand fast in the true grace of God." It conveys strength and consolation to Christians under stress.

Although Roman persecution may not have spread worldwide, the writer certainly anticipates that possibility. This may be the background in the latter part of the book (1 Pet. 4:12–5:11). The suggestion to "stand fast in the true grace of God" would have special meaning in light of state persecution.

On the other hand, the first portion of the book may have been a baptismal sermon for new converts (1 Pet 1:–4:11). The phrases "put away" (putting off old clothes for the baptismal service and replacing them with white robes, symbolizing purity), "like newborn babes," drinking "pure spiritual milk" (after baptism) to "grow up to salvation," all may reflect a message to new converts.

The persecution the readers faced in this section of the message was likely a community persecution. In the face of community ridicule and harassment, they were advised to maintain good conduct among the Gentiles, so that in case anyone spoke against the believers as wrongdoers, the Gentiles would see their good deeds, "and glorify God on the day of salvation" (1 Pet. 2:12).

After calling upon the church to be "good stewards" during the time of suffering (1 Pet. 4:7–11), the writer concludes with a variety of exhortations and greetings (1 Pet. 5:1–14).

> "And after you have suffered a little while, the God of all grace, who has called you to his eternal glory in Christ, will himself restore, establish, and strengthen you."
> 1 Peter 5:10

Chapter Fifty-Nine

THE EFFORT TO LIVE

We were returning from a visit to a sick friend. My companion Gene Cole was blind. Unfamiliar with his neighborhood, I attempted to park at the sidewalk that lead directly into his apartment. It was not easy. All of the individual apartments looked alike, including the small front porch each one boasted. Stopping before one of them, my blind friend immediately began directing me, "You are not far enough forward. Pull up. No! Too much. Back up. A little more. That's it. You are right in front of my place," he said confidently. Proceeding to get out of the car, I hurried to say, "Wait, how in the world did you know that I was in front of your house and not someone else's apartment?" "Well," he replied, "if you'll notice, my street has a slow incline to it from corner to corner. I knew by the tilt of the car when you had rolled to the right place."

I was impressed, but I was even more impressed by what he had said in conversation on the way home. "Dying," he offered, "would be easy. I am ready to die right now. It is the living that is the hard part. It is difficult to live day in and day out." I officiated at his funeral recently and remembered his words.

Considering the end of all things, contemplating the second coming of Christ can be a quick substitute for the day by day task of living in faith. We have no control over the first matter. The prospect of the latter calls for a determined commitment and a daily effort to live. May you be greatly strengthened in your effort today. The grace of God be yours.

2 PETER

Most scholars think 2 Peter is a pseudonymous letter. Various factors point to a time period after Peter's life. Among them is the slowness of the early church, even reluctance to accept the book. This slowness and reluctance is seen in the following statements. It is totally different in style and character from 1 Peter. So much time has passed that people have abandoned hope in the Second Coming. The apostles are spoken of as figures of the past. Apparently the Apostle Peter has already died.

The letter is devoted to the problem of the delay of the Second Coming. It is a defense of Christian eschatology, or beliefs about the end times, directed mainly against Gnostic teachers and their denial of the return of Christ and any hope of the establishment of the Kingdom of God.

The scoffers of the time said, "For ever since the fathers fell asleep, all things have continued as they were from the beginning of creation" (2 Pet. 3:4). In response, the writer argues that this is not true, and he points to the flood in Genesis as an example (2 Pet. 3:6). Second, the writer reminds the reader that the timetable God uses is different from man's. ". . . with the Lord one day is as a thousand years, and a thousand years as one day" (2 Pet. 3:8). Third, the Second Coming is delayed as an act of God's mercy. "The Lord is not slow about his promise as some count slowness, but is forbearing toward you, not wishing that any should perish, but that all should reach repentance" (2 Pet. 3:9).

> "Have no anxiety about anything, but in everything by prayer and supplication with thanksgiving let your requests be made known to God, and the peace of God which passes all understanding will keep your hearts and minds in Christ Jesus."
> Philippians 4:6–7

Chapter Sixty
FACING THE STORM

The guitarist in the three-piece band sat casually with his legs sprawled, looking as though he would go to sleep while plucking his instrument. Between numbers, the master of ceremonies introduced him. "This is my brother," he said. "As you can tell, he is kind of laid back." Going over to the guitarist, the emcee said to him, "Brother, you don't worry much, do you?" "Naw I don't," he replied. "Well, how do you manage that?" the emcee questioned. "I have someone who does my worrying for me. When I got something to worry about, I just give it to him and he worries for me. I don't worry," said the guitarist. "How did you find someone to do that?" queried the emcee. "It's easy," replied his brother, "I just pay him one hundred thousand dollars a year, and he does my worrying for me." "Whoa!" the emcee exclaimed, "I know how much you make brother. How could you possibly pay someone one hundred thousand dollars?" "Oh," concluded the guitarist, "I let him worry about that."

Well, that's a novel idea. But most of us cannot afford it financially, and we can't afford it emotionally, either.

A long time ago, I heard how a herd of steers on the open range responded to a severe winter storm. The rancher discovered that many had walked with their backs to the icy winds and had been stopped by the barbed wire fence. There they died. But some of them apparently faced the storm and walked steadily into it. They survived.

It would be great if someone could effectively worry for us in the face of life's storms. Since that cannot be the case, facing and walking into the wind may be the first step, as we place our faith in God to see us through the storm. As John writes, "And this is the confidence which we have in him, that if we ask anything according to his will, he hears us. And if we know that he hears us in whatever we ask, we know that we have the requests made of him" (1 John 5:14–15).

1 JOHN

1 John may be more correctly called a tract or homily. It does not have the form of an epistle. It lacks a formal salutation. There is no identification of the ones to whom it is addressed, and the customary farewell is missing.

The author does not mention his name, but indicates that he writes in order that "our joy may be complete" (1 John 1:4). In this vein, he warns his readers "not to fall into sin" (1 John 2:1). Throughout the letter, he writes to deepen the spiritual lives of his readers. He sets tests of discipleship, which give criteria upon which the reader might base assurance of salvation and possession of eternal life. Some of the tests are "walking in the light" (1 John 1:7), "love of the brethren" (1 John 2:9–11), "faith in Jesus Christ as the Son of God" (1 John 2:23), "living a life of victory over sin" (1 John 3:4–10), and "recognizing the presence of God's Spirit in life" (1 John 3:24).

It is apparent that the church is in a period of struggle. It works to identify the false teachers who are the "liars," the "antichrists" (1 John 2:22), and those who do not confess that Jesus Christ has "come in the flesh" (1 John 4:1–3). Apparently it was a time of difficulty and stress in the church as it addressed these issues.

> "And now I beg you, lady, not as though I were writing you a new commandment, but the one we have had from the beginning, that we love one another."
> 2 John 5

Chapter Sixty-One
A NEIGHBORLY BILLBOARD

The billboard on the interstate read, ". . . that thing about loving your neighbor as yourself, I meant that.—God"

The world is full of good folks and some who are not so good. The necessity of identifying and avoiding the drug pusher, the abuser, the scam artist, the thief, the crook, and others of like kind is a fact of life. The challenge in the process is not to lump our neighbors into the group because they don't look like us or think exactly as we do. The easy thing to do is to assume they are not good folks. The right thing to do is to remember that they are neighbors, and that you are to love your neighbor as yourself.

2 JOHN

2 John seems to share the same troubled background in the church as does 1 John. It may or may not be by the same author.

The letter is apparently directed to a particular church. The recipient is designated as "the elect lady and her children . . ." (2 John 1:1).

The particular concern in the letter is the issue of showing hospitality to traveling missionaries. The author warns the church against giving hospitality to those who deny the humanity of Christ (2 John 1:7), and those who repudiate the deity of Christ (2 John 1:9). Such persons are not to be offered room and board as they travel through town.

> "Do not withhold good from those to whom it is due, when it is in your power to do it."
> Proverbs 3:27

Chapter Sixty-Two
DOING GOOD

If being hospitable includes doing good for other folks, then Marie Lofton was hospitable. She possessed a wonderfully simple but dynamic theology. She had little patience with splitting hairs over theological matters, or debating fine distinctions in doctrine, or classifying folks as right or wrong in matters of their thinking. Theology was practicing your faith. Marie was a practicing theologian, the only kind that made any sense to her. Like Jesus, about whom it was written, "He went about doing good," Marie wanted to do good. And she did—even in death, giving her body to Vanderbilt Hospital, she continued to do good. Her last selfless act will help the medical profession give help and better health to others. Walking hand in hand with the One who went about doing good, Marie will continue to do good for years to come.

In a day when we are hesitant to assist a stranded motorist, afraid to pick up a hitchhiker, reluctant to open the door to a foreign voice, and fearful of doing other hospitable acts we once took for granted, the need for hospitality continues. We are challenged to discover ways to make it work. Like Marie, we must find ways to do good. "He who does good is of God" (3 John 11).

3 JOHN

This letter also grew out of the same troubled time in the church as did the previous letter. It is addressed to Gaius, a member of the unknown church with the troubled background.

The message of 3 John is almost a correction of 2 John. If 2 John advocated withholding hospitality to traveling missionaries, 3 John reminds the readers to practice hospitality to legitimate missionaries. The writer takes Diotrephes to task because he did not extend such hospitality. The church is reminded through Gaius to continue doing good.

> "For he will hide me in his shelter in the day of trouble; he will conceal me under the cover of his tent; he will set me high upon a rock."
> Psalm 27:5

Chapter Sixty-Three

THE KEEPER

A baby still in the mother's womb certainly would not choose to be removed from its warm berth, secure in its familiar environment and procedures. Yet birth is a positive and developing experience for the baby. When the baby is grown, it finds a warm berth in the world, secure in a familiar environment. Confronted with leaving life behind in death, perhaps a grown-up would not choose to be removed. Yet, cannot death be another positive and developing experience? This may be the perspective taken by a well known children's prayer:

> Now I lay me down to sleep
> I pray the Lord my soul to keep.
> If I should die before I wake,
> I pray the Lord my soul to take.

This perspective is stated elegantly by Jude:

> Now to him who is able to keep you from falling and to present you without blemish before the presence of his glory with rejoicing, to the only God, our Savior through Jesus Christ our Lord, be glory, majesty, dominion, and authority before all time and now and for ever. Amen. (Jude 24–25)

May such strength be yours for the beginning and the close of life.

JUDE

The brief letter of Jude warns against false teachers and urges steadfastness in the faith, much like 2 Peter. This writer does not deal with doubts concerning the Second Coming like 2 Peter, however.

The false teachers are not easily identified, for the writer does not so much describe their teaching as he condemns the teachers. "These are blemishes on your love feasts, as they boldly carouse together looking after themselves; waterless clouds, carried along by winds, fruitless trees in late autumn, twice dead, uprooted; wild waves of the sea, casting up the foam of their own shame; wandering stars for whom the nether gloom of darkness has been reserved for ever" (Jude 12–13).

"Then the seventh angel blew his trumpet, and there were loud voices in heaven saying, 'The kingdom of the world has become the kingdom of our Lord and his Christ, and he shall reign for ever and ever.'"
Revelation 11:15

Chapter Sixty-Four

The Victory

The little group numbered about twenty. Gathered together in the nursing home livingroom, the devotional leader from a local church was about to address the group. Many had lost a mate, the children of some had died, and all had experienced four or more wars. Disease, illness, and injury had been the regular, if unwelcome, companions of life. Now some were becoming forgetful and most were confused much of the time.

What should or could the devotional leader say to such a group? The verse read came unexpectedly from the book of Revelation. The words were, "The kingdom of the world has become the kingdom of our Lord and of his Christ, and he shall reign for ever and ever" (11:15).

The Lord is in control of the world. It is his. He created it and it is his domain. Everything is going to be all right. God is going to take care of you. The victory over life is his, and because it is his, it is also yours.

No one knows how much of the devotion was retained by the group. But no matter the circumstances we live under, the words of Revelation 11:15 and the victory are intended to be ours.

REVELATION

The book can be characterized as a letter, addressed to seven churches. It can be thought of as a prophecy (Rev. 1:3). It can be viewed as a great drama. Some commentators have accepted drama as a proper clue to its interpretation. And lastly, it is spoken of as an apocalypse or revelation (Rev. 1:1).

The last characterization probably has caused the most difficulty in interpretation. As a type of literature, apocalyptic writing arose about 200 B.C. and flourished until about 200 A.D. After the passing of the prophets, the times were evil, messianic salvation did not appear, and the Jews suffered untold persecutions. This gave rise to a literature which purported to bring revelations from God, explaining the reason for the presence of evil, disclosing the secrets taking place in heavenly courts, and promising the imminent coming of God's kingdom and the salvation of the oppressed and suffering faithful. Evil, which was intensely powerful, was confronted and overcome when God personally addressed it.

The apocalyptic writers used a particular set of tools to tell their story. The tools consisted of numbers used as symbols (numerology), animal symbolism, and pictures of strange creatures, having a combination of human and beastly or birdlike qualities. Colors were used (white for conquest, pale for death, etc.). Striking imagery was used and poetic description was paramount. The catastrophic woes before the end of an age, as well as visions and other writing tools, have all caused confusion for the interpreter. Underneath the multiple pictures created by the tools was a strikingly singular message. Those to whom it was directed understood it. They understood the need to camouflage the powerful message in a bewildering array of unusual pictures. It was to protect those to whom it was directed from the wrath of that first century beast, the Roman Empire.

The apocalyptic challenge is compounded by the question of whether Revelation should be approached literally, allegorically, dramatically, as a detailed forecast of history, or primarily as the end of history. The reader is justifiably confused about which approach he should take. It would be helpful if another example of apocalyptic writing could be read before reading Revelation. Nevertheless, which approach should be taken?

There are many approaches, each one earnestly and exhaustively taken by a host of interpreters. However, it would seem that a sound approach would assume that the author addressed the

Christians of a particular area in a time of danger. Moreover, one great theme was at the heart of apocalyptic writing. It was written to encourage faithful followers in times of trouble. The literary tools used were window dressings for the dominant message. The purpose of the writings was never meant to confuse or discourage the reader. In Revelation, the writer (identified only as John) intended to encourage Christians to be faithful to Christ, even unto death. John used visions and images, but he spoke a clear message to a first century generation of Christians. He did this just as other writers in the New Testament did. His message was that in Christ, there is victory over the world (Rev. 11:15). As is the case with the New Testament in general, this is a timeless message. Its message is for the church in all generations, and for all times of persecution and trouble:

> The kingdom of the world has become the kingdom of our Lord and his Christ, and he shall reign for ever and ever (Rev. 11:15).

About the Author

Clyde Willis Cutrer Sr. is a native of Kentwood, Louisiana. A graduate of Louisiana State University and the Southern Baptist Theological Seminary, he completed his doctoral studies at Vanderbilt University. A Baptist pastor for twenty-four years, Cutrer has spent the last twenty years teaching at Belmont University in Nashville, Tennessee, where he was recently named professor emeritus in religion. He has two grown children and lives in Madison, Tennessee, with his wife, Helen.